GOD SENSE

GOD
Sense

*Reading the Bible
for Preaching*

PAUL SCOTT WILSON

Abingdon Press
Nashville

GOD SENSE: READING THE BIBLE FOR PREACHING

This book is printed on acid-free paper.

Library of Congress Cataloging-in-Publication Data
Wilson, Paul Scott, 1949-
  God sense: reading the Bible for preaching / Paul Scott Wilson.
    p. cm.
  Includes bibliographical references and index.
  ISBN 0-687-00632-5 (acid-free paper)
    1. Bible—Homiletical use. I. Title.

BS534.5 .W56 2001
220.6'01—dc21

2001046095

01 02 03 04 05 06 07 08 09 10—10 9 8 7 6 5 4 3 2 1

MANUFACTURED IN THE UNITED STATES OF AMERICA

Contents

PART I
LITERAL READINGS:
HISTORICAL AND THEOLOGICAL CRITICISM

PART II
SPIRITUAL READINGS:
HOMILETICAL CRITICISM

Foreword

Preachers need distinctive ways to read the Bible that are not much acknowledged or discussed. This project provides preachers and students with responsible ways to recover theological reading of the Bible for homiletics. By learning to use theology for effective biblical interpretation, preachers discover things in texts that they did not see before and are enabled to preach in creative and powerful new ways that serve the gospel and engage the congregation. Our teachers for these ways of reading are our preaching ancestors through the ages.

Preachers often assume that the knowledge of biblical exegesis they gain in seminary is fully adequate biblical preparation for the pulpit. Exegetical method typically gets at history and literary matters, yet by and large it does not often get to theology and faith— in other words to the Bible as Scripture. Our ancestors pioneered theological ways of reading the Bible that address how the Bible functions for the church. They allowed the text to make effective connections with God, other biblical texts, church doctrine, and the congregation.

Most books dealing with our critical heritage and preaching, like Leander Keck's classic, *The Bible in the Pulpit* (Abingdon Press, 1978), confine their study to the present or to the period since the Reformation. If we want to understand the roots of our biblical interpretative strategies, however, we do well to go back to the patristic "four senses" of Scripture since they are devised for preachers. By better understanding how we come to do what we do, we can speak with greater confidence about what is needed in our age.

These classic senses represent a missing chapter in most of our education as preachers. They also constitute how Scripture is interpreted by our preaching forebears for the first fifteen hundred years of the church's life and, with considerable correction and evolution, how we as preachers interpret Scripture today though we may be loathe to admit it. The fourfold senses remain a consistent norm to the Reformation. By examining them we begin to read the Bible in fresh ways and open doors that previously have been shut out of neglect, fear, or simply out of difficulty in comprehending an approach to Scripture that seems so foreign to our own. The ancient senses become for us lenses with which to reconceive how we find the sermon in the Bible. Most important, they help us rediscover God in the Bible, not that God was missing, but our ways of reading have not always led us to God.

The main purpose of this book is to help preachers and students be more creative and faith-centered in reading the Bible for preaching. Thus to clarify our approach to the Bible in homiletics, I devise parallel biblical tasks under the rubrics of three kinds of criticism: historical, theological, and homiletical. Readers are instructed in three kinds of imagination appropriate to each. A secondary purpose of this project is to help preachers reclaim their preaching roots. I write as a preacher and professor of homiletics; thus what is found here belongs to practical theology.

I owe my thanks to many people in the completion of this project, and as usual my first and greatest debt is to my wife, Deanna, for her love and patience as well as for her interest in the subject and her helpful questioning that added much to the clarity of my own thought. I also owe thanks to my students at the basic degree and doctoral levels at the Toronto School of Theology who always teach me so much; to Roger Hutchinson, Principal of Emmanuel College; and to the President and Board of Regents of Victoria University in the University of Toronto for their support during a sabbatical leave. I am also deeply grateful to many individuals and committees responsible for several events that allowed me to test some of these ideas, in particular: the John N. Gladstone Festival of Preaching at McMaster Divinity College, Hamilton, Ontario; the 2000 Tipple-Vosburgh Lectures at Drew University Theological School; the Preaching Workshop at Wartburg Theological Seminary; and the Jameson Jones Lectures in Preaching at Duke Divinity School. Finally, I owe a debt of thanks to several colleagues in the Academy of Homiletics who kindly volunteered to read the manuscript and make important contributions to its final form and content, though they are unable to alter deficiencies of my own that remain: Stephen Farris, Joseph R. Jeter, John M. Rottman, and Art Van Seters.

CHAPTER ONE

Reading Scripture with Many Lenses

How can preaching be revitalized? Look at the preaching sites on the Internet, and there is no shortage of suggestions—everything from borrowing someone else's sermon to subscribing to on-line preaching journals. Look to preaching shelves in the library and the range of suggestions is no less wide, everything from disguising the sermon as a talk to conceiving of yet new forms to try. Preaching needs to be biblical, and one of the best ways for us as preachers to produce stronger sermons is to pay better attention to what we do with the Bible in preaching. We need new lenses, new spectacles to allow us to see things in the text that we have not seen before and to present them in our sermons.

In physics, light passes through a lens and is bent or is otherwise altered by it. Something similar to the refraction of light happens every time we read any text; the lens we use affects how we see it and what it says. Different lenses enable us to view some things even as they prevent us from viewing others. Anytime we receive new lenses for reading Scripture, our capacity to appreciate it increases. They allow us to read familiar texts in new ways and to discover how the texts themselves point to new and creative possibilities for sermons. Not any lens will do; in fact, among the best new lenses are ones that are actually very old—lenses that were designed by our preaching forebears, yet that fell out of favor along the historical path and are forgotten. Here we take them up again to adapt them to our own purposes of proclaiming God in creative and powerful ways.

The Genius of Our Ancestors

Our ancestors were brilliant. When they interpreted Scripture, they noticed that they made four kinds of theological comments.

They thus devised and regularized four ways of speaking about biblical texts that they called the four senses or meanings of Scripture (not to be confused with our five physical senses). A text literally describes a historical event, hence the literal sense; a text implies theological doctrine, hence the allegorical sense; a text calls for a change in how life is lived, hence the moral sense; and a text implies something about the next life, hence the prophetic sense. Early and medieval preachers picked up these four senses like four different pairs of eyeglasses, used them to read the Bible, and thereby discovered four different kinds of things to say about a lesson for their sermons. So reliable were these glasses that they passed them on from generation to generation for fifteen hundred years, and they provided the basis for biblical interpretation and preaching through to the reformers.

Our preaching forebears perceived relative theological completeness in these four senses that allowed them (1) to read the Bible as the church's book, (2) to read Scripture as a means to see Christ, and (3) to read Scripture as a way to look at ourselves. Early preachers conceived of the senses in an age that had no systematic theology or any means of relating the Old Testament and the New. Without these senses, the Old Testament could not be preserved as Christian Scripture and the New Testament could not be understood as a witness to the same God. Fourfold interpretation was a key factor in the conversion of many people including Augustine, who found in it a means to appreciate Scripture in line with his background in rhetoric and philosophy. Moreover, the four senses provided meanings of texts that otherwise were in doubt, allowed connections to be made among different biblical texts, and thereby provided a foundation with which systematic theology could develop.

Multiple senses were the most scientific tools available and much early and medieval interpretation was sophisticated. Because our own tools for reading Scripture have moved considerably beyond those of our patristic and medieval forebears, we should not assume that they were less rigorous, committed, or faithful in reading the Bible than we are. (Indeed, a few centuries from now, our approaches might be viewed as curious.) In fact, our own age largely fails where our ancestors excelled: They understood that the Bible deals in revelation and that Scripture from beginning to end is about God and God's relationships to humanity and the rest of creation. The multiple senses were not strictly limited to four in the early and medieval church, and our study speaks of many lenses, and some within others much in the manner that we have bifocal and trifocal lenses. We are tempted to think of theological lenses as "applications" of Scripture to particular doctrinal, ethical, and prophetic purposes. This way of thinking betrays our modern mind-set. For the ancients, spiritual meanings were inherent in the text as part of the divine Author's intention: God puts them there and is speaking them now. Texts for them had literal and grammatical significance in history, yet they had direct significance for their own contemporary time in and through the Holy Spirit, who guarantees their meaning.

What Can We Hope to Learn from Fourfold Exegesis?

One key benefit to be derived from the four senses of Scripture is the recovery for preaching of a lively sense of Scripture that focuses upon God and God's purposes for humanity and creation. We can speak of the four senses as four lenses for us, yet we can also speak of the four senses as one theological lens with differing levels that brings the Bible into focus as God's Word. Biblical criticism today, in spite of recent improvements, tends to affirm historical meanings of Scripture at the expense of theological. This must not prevent preachers from affirming theological meanings that conform to how the church understands Scripture. In particular, preachers need a creative process that uses theological imagination to communicate God, God's action in the past and present, and the promise of God's actions in the future. Preachers need to recover the God sense of Scripture.

A second benefit is appreciation of the ongoing importance of history in discovering what the text actually says—literal meanings in a text. Historical imagination offers creative skills to visualize biblical events and to put them before the congregation in exciting ways. Historical-critical study of the Bible is currently under attack from various quarters, in spite of its strength in recovering the Bible as a historical document. On one hand some critics are frustrated with its apparent incapacity to respond to the Bible as Scripture, as the Word of God. On the other hand, some critics want to reject traditional critical approaches entirely in favor of various kinds of literary interpretation like deconstruction and reader response. Whatever promise these newer approaches hold in opening fresh ways to understand biblical texts, they also destabilize texts and undermine their authority as Scripture for the church. Historical approaches remain essential for preaching to ensure that the meanings we find in Scripture are rooted in biblical events.

Since we no longer employ the four senses, scholars assume that they are dead and gone. In fact, they have evolved into homiletical criticism. A third benefit of this project is a practice to interpret the Bible using homiletical criticism: to make connections to congregations; to identify situations in our own world that the text addresses; to call forth actions of love and justice in regard to those situations; to name doctrines that reinforce textual understandings; and to point to where all things finally lead in God's great plan. For this a third kind of imagination is needed: Homiletical imagination portrays the people in the Bible and our world as real people to whom we determine appropriate theological, pastoral, and ethical response.

A fourth benefit is a more effective conception of sermon preparation that will result in stronger preaching. Each of the various ways preachers read the Bible can be fairly represented and apportioned time in the homiletical process. Preachers benefit by engaging throughout the week these three kinds of critical and imaginative approaches: historical, theological, and homiletical. This goes against what preachers typically are taught: Perform scholarly study of the biblical text and then select a homiletical form to be filled with content. Some preachers unfortunately spend most of their preparation time doing historical-critical study of the Bible and never get to theological and homiletical interpretation. Our ancestors knew that biblical interpretation did not happen at one stage followed by homiletics—biblical interpretation is intimately connected with every stage of homiletical endeavor from beginning to end. Historical criticism is the start, to be sure, yet it is also engaged simultaneously with theological and homiletical criticism. They operate on parallel tracks. Without all three, the fullness of the gospel cannot effectively be proclaimed. In other words, biblical interpretation is finished only when the sermon is delivered, and traditional teaching about biblical interpretation does not take us nearly as far as it should. In this regard, preachers have ways of reading Scripture that are distinctive from yet complementary to the work of many scholars upon whom they rely.

A fifth benefit concerns the poetry implied in the four senses. They are not only a way of viewing Scripture, or of finding meaning when meaning seems elusive; they are also a way of reading the world, for the God who wrote Scripture also inscribes truth in the blowing winds, in the greening meadows, and throughout all nature. Scripture texts interconnect with one another and with nature and point to one unified truth of Christ.[1] Our ancestors saw more harmony and unity in life than we are sometimes able to find in our postmodern world. For them, all life was like converging streams and rivers that flow with minor interruption toward one great common goal: God's purpose of salvation. Hugh of St. Victor, for example, marvels that in the mathematical progression 1-3-9-27-81 . . . , every fourth number contains the number one.[2] He reads God's intention into such patterns and marvels at God's wisdom in a manner that may seem strange to us until we remember that scientists who explore the origins of the universe or of DNA today commonly refer to God to account for the intelligence they discover. One does not have to hunt far for God in the medieval world because there is a surplus of divine meaning in everything; one simply needs gifts of discernment. As Hugh says, "By contemplating what God has made we realize what we ourselves ought to do. Every nature tells of God; every nature teaches man; every nature reproduces its essential form, and nothing in the universe is infecund."[3] Although our age is highly suspicious of authority and a single view of the world when many are available, we can still strive for greater focus on God in our lives and greater integration of our worldviews centered in God, Scripture, and theology.

Why the Four Senses Are Discarded

Preachers of old discovered allegory to be a way to connect with other texts, with the teachings of the church, and with congregations. This simple means of connection said, "this text means this" or "this is this." Allegory afforded a freedom and creativity to proclaim the gospel and to defend Scripture from attack. Of course that same freedom also led to the downfall of allegory, for it was open to abuse: Interpreters read their own prejudices into Scripture and claimed they were the text's actual meaning. Misuse of allegory contributed to terrible, tragic chapters of anti-Semitism and racial and religious intolerance in Christian history; thus, allegory poses particular problems for us when we strive to learn from it. Unfortunately some preachers today still use allegory as a way of saying that texts mean what they do not mean, and they thereby distort the gospel message. Biblical texts are used by these preachers as a simple framework upon which to hang their own private understandings and beliefs. It is no wonder that those of us who teach and preach are highly alert to allegory as an abuse of Scripture wherever it appears. It represents a continuing danger in biblical exegesis and the pulpit, partly because allegorical interpretation is so easy to fall into and tends to threaten what the church affirms as the real meaning of Scripture.

Of course, any lens is open to abuse. The literal lens is as prone to error as allegory. Literal interpretation claims, for example, that "all nations" are to be baptized (Matt. 28:19) encouraged the Spanish Inquisition; that the Jews killed Jesus (Matt. 27:23) contributes to anti-Semitism and, perhaps, ultimately contributed to the holocaust; that slaves are to be obedient to their masters (e.g., Eph. 6:5; 1 Tim. 6:1-5) buttressed the colonial slave trade and apartheid in South Africa; that women are to be obedient to their husbands (Col. 3:18) contributes to the oppression of women; and that people are to have dominion over all living things (Gen. 1:28) gives license to the destruction of thousands of the Earth's species and the degradation of the environment. Still, we do not reject the literal sense because it has this destructive potential when abused.

We rightly reject the practice of bad allegory, yet in doing so we end up throwing out the entire principle of it. Not all allegory is bad. In discarding allegory we also trash the four senses that some people associate with it, even though they provide so many important contributions to what is good in Christian heritage. Although we probably cannot use the term, allegory continues to be the means whereby we make connections with other biblical texts, doctrines, and congregational needs today. If we are not doing this, the text is not functioning as Scripture for the church. Instead of continuing to use allegory as a generic symbol for all that is bad in interpretation, we should concentrate our efforts on being more precise about what we mean and on identifying good and bad uses of allegory for preaching.

Where Do the Multiple Senses of Scripture Originate?

Early Christians did not invent the multiple senses, they were already present in ancient Greek and Jewish hermeneutics. Greek scholars developed spiritual interpretations of Homer, thinking him to be divinely inspired.[4] In the century before Christ, Philo the Jew identified two senses in Jewish Scriptures: the literal that has to do with the letters of the text, and the spiritual that has to do with the real meaning of the text. He used these in an analogy to the body and soul and recommended the spiritual sense as the more important, for it represented "the invisible intention latent in the text."[5]

Christians adopted and developed the tradition of senses in part because they found experiences in the Old Testament that paralleled their own and afforded them the promise of deeper understanding. They also adopted the senses because they could not understand many of the passages taken at face value. Paul occasionally uses allegory, the most notorious of the multiple senses. Scholars often point to Paul speaking of Hagar and Sarah as the two covenants, where Hagar corresponds to the earthly Jerusalem and Sarah to the heavenly city (Gal. 4:21-31). Paul gives primary impetus to spiritual interpretation in the early church when he writes that the Corinthians are "ministers of a new covenant, not of letter but of spirit; for the letter kills, but the Spirit gives life" (2 Cor. 3:6). By this the early church understood that the letter *(Gk. grámma)* or literal interpretation kills in that it misses the spiritual significance of the text. Origen extends Philo's analogy of the body: the literal (flesh or body) sense helps simple, common people avoid error, the moral (psychological or soul) sense awakens the human soul to ethical life, and the spiritual (intellectual, allegorical, or prophetic) sense brings enlightened individuals into union with God and doctrinal truth.[6] In practice, Origen tends to use only the literal and spiritual senses.

Over the years, scholars have varied the number and identity of these senses. Augustine, for example, speaks of four senses of

Scripture,[7] two of which are not in Origen. The standard exegetical model that became known as the fourfold method or *quadriga* was provided by John Cassian, Chrysostom's deacon, in his *Conferences*, which later became required reading for the Benedictine Rule (ca. 529) and had enormous influence on preaching because it guided monastic life in the west. His four senses are what we identified earlier: the literal, the allegorical, the moral, and the prophetic. He offers a famous example of the four meanings of "Jerusalem" as it is found in various places in Scripture: Literally it is the actual city; allegorically it is the church (e.g., Ps. 46:5, "God is in the midst of the city"); morally it is the human soul (e.g., Ps. 147:2-3, "The LORD builds up Jerusalem. . . . He heals the brokenhearted"); and prophetically it is the heavenly city of God (e.g., Gal. 4:26, "Jerusalem . . . is our mother").[8]

A Scandinavian Dominican, Augustine of Dacia (d. 1281), composed a rhyme that was intended to serve as a memory device for preachers, and, with a slight variation by Nicholas of Lyra, it became standard for the Middle Ages:

> *Littera gesta docet, quid credas allegoria,*
> *Moralis quid agas, quo tendas anagogia.*[9]

> The letter teaches events
> allegory what you should believe
> tropology what you should do
> anagogy where you should aim.[10]

An English paraphrase gives an additional perspective:

> The letter shows us what God and our fathers did;
> The allegory shows us where our faith is hid;
> The moral meaning gives us rules of daily life;
> The anagogy shows us where we end our strife.[11]

When we see the word "spiritual" we should think of the word "theological," for all three of the spiritual senses (allegorical, moral, and prophetic) offer theological meanings of texts. We can see this in an early fourteenth-century letter to Can Grande, once thought to be written by Dante, that interprets the Exodus literally as the historical journey; allegorically as salvation in Christ; morally as individual conversion from sin; and prophetically as the journey of the soul to spiritual union with Christ.[12] All three of the spiritual senses also immediately speak to daily life and belief. Together, they provide preachers with a means to discover what there is to say about a subject and a means to proclaim the fullness of the gospel while being faithful to specific texts.

Three Keys to Fourfold Exegesis

Three of the early church doctrinal understandings provide a key to the multiple senses: the doctrines of plenary or verbal inspiration of Scripture, the doctrine of the unity of Scripture, and the doctrine of the Fall.

1. *Plenary or Verbal Inspiration of Scripture.* Our ancient ancestors typically understood Scripture to be completely inspired, word for word, and the multiple senses were a gift God provided as a means of unlocking biblical truth. We must nonetheless be careful not to read rationalist theories of verbal inspiration back into the early church, for their exegesis and interpretation, like that of the Jewish tradition, was rich, flexible, and imaginative. In their understanding, the Scriptures descended from heaven and were transcribed as the dictation of God by humans whose own contributions were not recognized. God spoke in a code that could be understood properly only by those having the appropriate knowledge and spiritual insight. Scripture itself testified to its own rich potential and gave license for its own spiritual mining: "All scripture is inspired by God and is useful for teaching, for reproof, for correction, and for training in righteousness" (2 Tim. 3:16).

Today, when we encounter contradictions or apparent conflicting statements in a biblical text or it fails in other ways to make obvious sense, we look for some historical or cultural information to provide an explanation, or to the hand of a biblical editor who may have altered the text. The ancients used such textual conflict as a signal to look for higher spiritual meanings. Origen cites Isaiah 6:9-10 to prove that everyone is not intended to understand Scripture (*On First Principles*, Book IV): "Go and say to this people: 'Keep listening, but do not comprehend; keep looking, but do not understand.' Make the mind of this people dull, and stop their ears, and shut their eyes, so that they may not look with their eyes, and listen with their ears, and comprehend with their minds, and turn and be healed." God conceals truth from those not suited for it and discloses it only to those who are chosen. The goal of human life is spiritual growth and development, and the goal of studying the Bible similarly is to move beyond the literal sense of scriptural words in order to arrive at the higher spiritual meaning God intended.

2. *The Doctrine of the Unity of Scripture.* From the time of the early church, people understood Scripture to form a unity in that it testifies to one God and to the unity of God's will and actions.[13] God is not whimsical and unpredictable, acting this way in one moment and that way in another; nor is there one God of wrath in the Old Testament and another God of love in Paul, as Marcion claims. Rather, God has a unified will and purpose for humanity and acts toward humans in ways that are consistent with it. Scripture testifies to this unity in various ways, not least through affirming that God cannot speak deceitfully or lie (2 Sam. 7:28; John 17:17; Heb. 6:18). The multiple senses are remarkable hermeneutical instruments that provided the early church with a way to understand Christ in light of the Hebrew Scriptures; to understand the Hebrew Scriptures in the light of Christ and thereby to preserve the Old Testament for Christian life and faith; to defend Scripture from attack; and to defend monotheism in spite of differences between Old and New Testaments. The ongoing life of the community of faith makes similar testimony. Revelation is often hidden in Scripture, yet because the biblical message is consistent and forms a unity, simple meanings in one place can be used to unlock difficult meanings elsewhere (a practice known as the analogy of faith, or its relative, the analogy of Scripture).

3. *The Doctrine of the Fall.* The multiple senses are a means of compensating for what was lost in the Fall. God's plan is evident in both the natural created order and in Scripture, which God dictated word by word for human benefit. Because of the Fall, humans cannot fully comprehend what God says, and God therefore adapts what is said to our deficient abilities. Some scholars identify this idea as the foundation of all medieval biblical interpretation.[14] God is inerrant, and since God planned everything in nature and Scripture, even the means of a decoding standard such as the multiple senses is part of God's intent. Scripture makes sense, has

meaning, and gives life; and if it fails in this regard, Scripture is not at fault; human sin is responsible. Apparent problems in Scripture point to deficiencies in understanding, and the interpreter's task is to make sense of the text as it stands. Through the multiple senses, God restores to humanity a means of comprehending God's saving purposes and of growing in spiritual insight.

The Arrangement of This Book

This book is divided into two parts: The first deals with the literal senses of Scripture and the second deals with the spiritual senses, which for our time we will call theological senses. The literal deserves an entire section because from the time of the reformers it has been regarded as the only sense of Scripture with which to argue doctrine and morality. Chapter 2 explores our exegetical method and how it has come to define what is the literal meaning for us; it demonstrates in practical ways how historical imagination needs to function for preachers. Chapter 3 shows that what the reformers understood and intended by the literal is not what we understand, for they had a higher theological literal sense in mind. Chapters 4 and 5 are practical chapters that deal with how we should now conceive of the literal sense and how we might conceive of theological exegesis for preachers, using theological imagination in reading Scripture.

Part 2 explores how the other ancient senses, though banished, continue to function in homiletics. These ancient spiritual senses are further theological senses that provide homiletical tools for theological interpretation of the Bible. All of these meanings reside within the biblical texts themselves, and without them the Bible cannot function as Scripture. Each of these later chapters thus contributes to what we mean by homiletical imagination. Chapter 6 examines the merits of reading texts for moral purpose and provides practical advice for preachers. Chapter 7 explores the role of allegory in history, and chapter 8 examines both allegory and prophecy (anagogy) from a practical preaching perspective, demonstrating how they are still needed and used by preachers though they go by different names.

Our pre-Reformation ancestors had obvious faults in their approach to Scripture, yet they also had some remarkable insights that continue as the unacknowledged backbone of our own methods of interpretation. Our purpose here is not to recover their way of handling Scripture but rather to approach Scripture seeking to find the same things they found: a connection with God, direction for life, understanding about Christ, and reason for hope. They had a strong understanding that Scripture is about God; they grasped the God sense of it. Our ancestors had good impulses in this regard, even if their methods were flawed. At least three of the words they used are loaded words in our theological community—literal, moral, and allegorical. Literal implies literalistic, moral implies moralistic, and allegory implies bad interpretation. Perhaps these words cannot be revived, yet they are so central to what preachers have done through the centuries that it seems unwise just to leave them by the side of the road.

Typically in seminaries the four senses are not taught. A change in attitude is overdue.[15] Our awareness of our heritage often goes back only to the Enlightenment or the Reformation and we remain largely ignorant of the ancient senses and the mind-set that spawned them, though often this is the same mind-set that gave us the Scriptures themselves. By writing off biblical interpretation prior to 1500, we invariably write off that preaching as well and count it as misguided. While such thinking may be understandable, we are presumptuous to dismiss so readily what God chose to accomplish in and through that preaching, as though for all the faults of our ancestors they were not also preaching the living Word of God as they were led by the Holy Spirit.

PART I
Literal Readings:
Historical and
Theological Criticism

"The letter shows us what God and our fathers did."
—Augustine of Dacia

CHAPTER TWO

The Literal Sense and Historical-Critical Exegesis

The purpose of this chapter is to explore the term "literal" and to show how historical-critical method comes to define literal in our day by squeezing out theological understandings of the text. One of the most widely accepted principles in homiletics, and one of the most reliable, is that the sermon, or homily, is based upon a biblical text. Scripture is at the heart of what Christians do, say, and are. Even the symbolism in worship, of a Bible in plain view and of reading from it, reinforces that we are a people of the Book, that this Book guides our lives, and that this Word being spoken is different in nature from other words. However, saying we preach the Bible does not clarify matters as much as one might hope. As Stephen Farris says, "There are . . . textual sermons that are profoundly unbiblical and nontextual sermons that are truly biblical."[1] What does it mean to preach the Bible? At least since the Reformation in the West, preaching the Bible means preaching the literal text, or, more precisely the literal meaning of the text. The word "literal" itself means "having to do with letters of the alphabet," thus the literal meaning of a biblical text is its obvious or plain meaning. The literal is sometimes understood in contrast to the figurative meanings of a text, its metaphors, similes, and other figures of speech, although commonly these are included in it since they too can be the plain meaning. The literal is opposed to allegory and other forms of impressionistic or theological interpretation that claim hidden or coded meanings imbedded in a text awaiting discovery by an educated or spiritual elite.

If we use the term "literal," we use it to claim that the interpretation we give to a text is what it actually says, not what we might arbitrarily read into it. The term "literal sense" of a biblical text can be conceived as (a) the plain meaning of the text. Second Peter 1:20 reads, "[N]o prophecy of scripture is a matter of one's own interpretation." "The Second Helvetic Confession" comments, "[T]he Holy Scriptures are not of private interpretation (II Peter 1:20), and thus we do not allow all possible interpretations."[2] The Bible is a public book that anyone can read or hear with benefit and understanding, thus "The Westminster Confession of Faith" reads: "All things in Scripture are not alike plain in themselves, nor alike clear unto all; yet those things which are necessary to be known, believed, and observed, for salvation, are so clearly propounded and opened in some place of Scripture or other that not only the learned but the unlearned, in a due use of the ordinary means, may attain unto a sufficient understanding of them."[3]

Sometimes the literal refers to the letters, grammar, and syntax of a text, thus the term "the grammatical sense" of the text is used. Sometimes the literal sense is identified as the "historical sense," communicating information about history and events as they actually happened. Sometimes a combination of terms is used (literal-grammatical, literal-historical, historical-grammatical), yet they all refer to this plain or public meaning that serves as a means to guarantee the historical authenticity of a text's meaning.

In addition, throughout history the literal meaning is conceived as (b) what the church understands the text to mean theologically and from the perspective of faith. From the early church, those who advocate on behalf of the literal text do not regard the sense of "the letter" or the grammatical-historical meaning as the destination of the preacher, it is simply the means to it. The preacher aims for the literal meaning that communicates Jesus Christ. This dual understanding of "literal" as history and as theology is common in history, yet it is lost in the Enlightenment. This is precisely the understanding preachers need to recover for more powerful preaching today.

Before we discuss this in detail, we need to consider first some typical understandings of "literal," the "literal sense," and the "literal text" that can prevent us from hearing what our ancestors have to say and second to identify how the "literal sense" relates to the scholarly study of biblical texts known as exegesis. Consider five common ideas that cause difficulty concerning the literal and preaching:

1. Literal translations are not literal. We assume that a literal translation follows the original text letter for letter and word for

word. Gregory the Great, along with most medieval scholars, held that the text was still the text even in translation. Scholars since Aristotle have understood that words can be altered while the meaning remains the same. However, since the Romantic age, this substitution theory of language has lost favor. Gerhard von Rad once cautioned, "Not a single word in the ancient language exactly coincides with the corresponding word in our language."[4] An introductory essay at the beginning of a new translation of the Bible commonly indicates the choice translators have had to make. Do they remain as close to the original as possible, preserving the sentence order and as much grammatical structure as possible, a method known as "formal equivalence" that strives for word-for-word translation, as is found, for instance, in the King James Version and the sometimes painfully literal American Standard Version? Or do they render the text most closely as it would be expressed and understood today, a process known as "functional" or "dynamic equivalence"? Inevitably any translation will use a combination of both approaches.

Dynamic equivalence strives for thought-for-thought translation. Arguments exist on either side as to which is most helpful. The editors of the New Living Translation maintain that their own dynamic approach "has the potential to represent the intended meaning of the original text even more accurately than a word-for-word translation."[5] Thus 1 Kings 2:10 in the KJV reads "So David slept with his fathers, and was buried in the city of David"; the NIV reads, "Then David rested with his fathers and was buried in the City of David"; and their own translation reads, "Then David died and was buried in the City of David." Of course one can still argue that these changes are relatively insignificant and that even when scholars dispute some phrases the meaning is not entirely in conflict or in question. The point is simply that even what we consider to be a literal translation is an interpretation. No reading of Scripture is unaffected by human hands.

2. Preachers claim to preach "the literal text" and speak as though the literal text is present in the sermon when it is not. The reformers understood their doctrines as biblical, almost to be the Bible in other words. To preach a Bible verse was to preach a doctrine, and to preach a doctrine was to preach something imbedded in the literal sense of many texts. "The Second

Helvetic Confession" understands this unity between Scripture and preaching as a continuation of the event of revelation and the self-communication of God, that is, "The preaching of the Word of God is the Word of God."[6] The reformers also maintained that the Bible in translation is still the Bible—followers of Islam by contrast say of the Koran that its translations are only its meanings, not the book itself. "The Westminster Confession of Faith" says that the original languages are "authentical" and the final source of appeal in controversy and that they are to be translated into every language, "the word of God dwelling plentifully in all."[7]

As long as preachers in history held to Aristotle's substitution theory of language, they could substitute sermon points for biblical metaphors, ideas for textual images, and doctrines for Bible stories and still claim to be preaching the text. This understanding of language was radically challenged for the first time in the 1800s by the English and German Romantics who established that metaphors have their own way of communicating and cannot simply be traded for less poetic words in the hope of communicating the same thing. Their understanding is still having an impact in recent times, as part of a second wave of Romantic influence that began in the 1930s, as seen in Hans Frei's argument about the unique ability of biblical narratives to communicate their own messages in their own way that cannot be reduced to doctrinal propositions.[8]

We can argue that even when preachers quote a biblical text exactly in a sermon, the literal text is not in the sermon. The biblical text can be present in the sermon only in a manner of speaking. As soon as we translate it or say what it means we change it. Furthermore, even if we recite an entire pericope or unit of Scripture at length in the sermon, we take it out of its setting. When we remove it from its surrounding verses and from the book as a whole, we alter the original. The purpose of careful biblical exegesis, of course, is to help us compensate for these deficits and to claim nonetheless that we have captured the literal sense of the text so that we can apply it to contemporary life. Still, every time we approach a text we leave our fingerprints on it. Or to use our metaphor of the lens, every time we read a text, we read it through a lens that alters or bends its light.

Thus if we are to be strict, the literal biblical text exists only in the Bible, and only in the original language, and then perhaps only to the minds and hearts of that culture and time. For the same reason, biblical commentaries say many things about the literal text and add many things to it that remain distinct from it. What we have there and in the sermon falls outside of the literal text. We might do better to call it an "illusion" of the literal text, drawing on Eric Auerbach,[9] or a "trace" of it, drawing on Derrida, the literal text being present in its absence,[10] or an image, approximation, or reconstruction of it. This is not to criticize our common and important practice of citing the biblical text in a sermon. Rather it is to caution against simplistic assumptions about safeguarding the literal text. At best as preachers we offer an interpretation of the text, and we are judged on the adequacy of that representation. It is not the only interpretation possible, nor is it the only legitimate one. When we claim to preach the literal text, we always speak either imprecisely or figuratively. The literal text cannot be preached. We inevitably preach a historical and imaginative reconstruction of the text. Nonetheless, if the interpretation is valid, it can be conceived as the Word of God precisely because it is God's living word, as opposed to a passage on an unread page.

3. Literalism, an uncompromising adherence to the literal text, is commonly understood to be a strict "following of the letter." It is dangerous because every letter is given equal weight and there is no means for distinguishing what emphases in the text are most important. In fact what passes for literalism functions as a kind of fundamentalism rather than a true rendering of the literal— although literalism is not confined to the conservative fundamentalist movement. Paul Tillich makes a useful distinction between "natural literalism" and "conscious literalism."[11] Natural literalism accepts the Bible as factual, much as children receive it, and is akin to how it was read in the pre-Enlightenment era. Conscious literalism is the conscious adoption of fundamentalist ideas that govern how one reads the Bible. Fundamentalism arose in America in the twentieth century as a reaction against reading Scripture critically using historical method. This form of fundamentalism emphasized the inerrancy of Scripture in matters of faith and morals, as well as Scripture as literal history, for example concerning the manner of the Second Coming of Christ. This fundamentalism commonly

assumed that inspiration was sufficient to understand the literal meaning of a text without historical research and inquiry.

To Tillich's two categories we may add a third category, "unconscious literalism," to identify a similar phenomenon in the religious left, for instance, among scholars confident that they have arrived at the historical Jesus through a sifting of the text. Some members of the Jesus Seminar, for instance, seem uncompromising in the way in which they read Scripture and make radical claims concerning the nature and person of Jesus based on a method that is less than historical.[12] They impose a limit on how Jesus' words are to be understood. In other words charges of excessive literalism, or fundamentalism for that matter, can be made across the theological spectrum. This confusion between literalism and literal can be a good reason for trying to find a new term instead of literal sense. Still, the literal sense is so important a concept in church history that to jettison the term because of recent difficulties is shortsighted.

4. Literal interpretations of the Bible are not always possible. Scholars use some of the apparent contradictions and gaps in scriptural texts to discern the hand of different writers and editors in both prebiblical tradition (when the Bible had not yet taken shape) and in assembly of the canon. Genesis 6–8 is an obvious example, for the story of Noah has variations in the number of animals taken into the ark. Various prophecies have come to pass figuratively but not literally, just as Jesus phrased some of his commands figuratively, as obvious metaphors. Here are some examples of texts that scholars throughout history have had difficulty interpreting literally.[13]

- Isaiah 13:9-22 predicts the destruction of the earth when the Medes and Persians overthrow Babylon.
- Zephaniah 1:18 says that the whole land of Judah and Jerusalem will be consumed by the fire of God's anger from which no one will survive.
- Malachi 4:5 reads that Elijah must come before the day of the Lord.
- Ezekiel 37:25 predicts that "David shall be their prince forever."

- Matthew 17:9-10—Jesus' authority is challenged on the basis of Malachi, and Jesus responds that Elijah has already come in John the Baptist.
- Matthew 24:30—Jesus cites Daniel 7:13, "'the Son of Man coming on the clouds of heaven' with power and great glory," and says at 24:34 "Truly I tell you, this generation will not pass away until all these things have taken place." See also Mark 8:38 and 9:1.

5. The idea of the literal sense, far from being obvious and fixed (as "according to the letter" implies), changes with time, which is another reason some scholars want to drop it. Sandra M. Schneiders, for instance, says, "I am proposing that the term *textual meaning* replace what has been called, in the context of a more positivistic understanding of interpretation, 'the literal meaning.' It is nearly impossible to find an enlightening definition of 'literal meaning.'"[14] Her suggestion of the term textual meaning is positive, particularly since it escapes confusion that arises between literal sense and literalistic or fundamentalistic reading. However, it negates the term that the church has used from its beginning, and here we are trying to reestablish the continuity between preachers of old and preachers today. We cannot adequately understand our history and our present homiletical difficulty if we try switching boats midstream. Textual meaning is as open to misinterpretation as the literal sense: Whose meaning? How do we arbitrate competing claims? What do we mean by text?

What we understand by literal sense is not what the church through most of its history has understood. In the early and medieval church, the literal was not necessarily considered to be the most important sense. Reformers cited both Augustine (from the beginning of his commentary on Genesis that emphasizes the book as literal truth) and Aquinas to affirm the literal as the only authentic meaning of Scripture for doctrine, faith, and morals. The literal meaning has to do with Jesus Christ (Luther) or with the meaning the Holy Spirit illuminates (Calvin). When the reformers said that Scripture has only one meaning, they meant its literal meaning. The literal sense is a theological understanding of the text as opposed to simply a grammatical or historical understanding.

Throughout much of the Enlightenment and continuing largely to the present, the literal sense of a text is the single, "objective" historical sense, often stripped of faith. The results of the de-theologizing of the literal sense for preaching have been mixed. On the one hand, preachers are given more reliable texts, essential help in understanding them against their historical and cultural background, and a range of biblical commentaries and other scholarly resources. On the other hand, preachers are not given much help in connecting the literal meaning of the text to the faith of the church, much less to God. Such theological focus is seen as an "application" of theology to the text that violates the neutrality scholars must preserve. A host of biblical scholars and preachers have tried to develop a theological correction, from Karl Barth (in his revolutionary commentary *The Epistle to the Romans*) to Elizabeth Achtemeier, Brevard Childs, Walter Brueggemann and others. Still, scholars have not always been clear how to help preachers to distinguish between their historical and theological tasks.

These five ideas that cause difficulty concerning the "literal" might seem to discourage our attempt to revive insights from our forebears concerning the literal meaning of Scripture; alternatively these ideas underline the importance of the task and point, in particular, to how the "literal" relates to theology.

Exegetical Method

For what do we listen in studying a biblical text? Some people might think that we immediately start listening for God's voice speaking to us as a direct form of inspiration, much as Elijah heard the "still small voice" of God upon the mountain. God can, of course, speak to us at any time and by any means. Still, God is not at our bidding to save us from work, growth, and maturity in the faith; moreover, murderers, rapists, and people with evil intent, as well as the mentally ill claim to hear God's voice. We have, as safeguards, the Bible witness and the community of faith in discerning that what is claimed of God is authentic.

We do not listen to the text at this stage to hear what we should preach. We hear what the text says in its own time and place. Exegesis is a process of questioning a biblical text in a manner that helps the interpreter encounter it afresh and think it through, which culminates in an informed reading. Exegesis literally means "to lead out" as opposed to eisegesis, "to lead into" or read into a text something that is not there. We call our method of study historical-critical exegesis. It is historical because it uses principles of history developed since the Enlightenment that demand verifiable evidence, scientific procedures, and reasoned conclusions. It is critical because it involves critical inquiry, skillful analysis, and synthesis and tries to eliminate presuppositions or beliefs that interfere with a fair reading of the text. Historical criticism presumes loyalty to the text and has been followed in its broad outlines for many decades by nearly every biblical preacher. It reads a text through history (diachronically), and recently it has been supplemented by literary criticism that appreciates a text in its wholeness at the present time (synchronically).

Exegesis normally follows established steps, like any investigative procedure. Below is a fairly typical way of appropriating historical and literary critical method as a standard and essential means of studying the Bible in preparation to preach. It does not tell us everything to preach, but it does go a long way toward telling us what we can and cannot say about the biblical passage we are studying:[15]

1. Read and reread the text. Get to know it intimately. Like detectives arriving on a crime scene, as critics we assume that our initial knowledge of the text is incomplete. We look for details we might not have noticed before. Reading the text aloud is a good strategy for discovering new things. One of the ways to read aloud is to allow one's senses to be stimulated by the language of the text—imagine seeing what the words describe and hearing the sound of the words to determine where emphasis and pauses are needed. This is especially important as preparation for public reading. If time permits, and particularly if a series of sermons will be delivered from the same book of the Bible, the entire book should be read.

2. Answer basic historical questions about the text from evidence you find within it: Who wrote it? What can you say about the human author? To whom was it written? On what occasion? For what purpose? What is the theme of the entire book? What is the theme of the passage? How do the two connect? What was happening in Israel's (or the church's or the world's) history at this

time? What has just happened or is about to happen? Does this passage or book cause anything to happen?

3. Determine the boundaries of the text, as a detective determines the perimeters of a crime scene. For example, does the portion of the text being examined have unity and coherence on its own, or do you need to consider a larger section? Ideally, the passage should represent a complete unit of thought, and special care needs to be taken concerning where to begin and end it. If you use a lectionary that prescribes lessons for each Sunday, you may need to extend a reading to include additional verses. If the meaning of a text is altered radically by a short excerpt, should the larger selection be read, or are there good textual and historical reasons for leaving it as is? (Some of these questions will need to be addressed by broader reading, as in #9.) Strive to honor the context of the thought, and not to make the text say something else.

4. If possible, do your own translation of the passage and check other versions of the Bible to see how others have translated the passage. With the original language, look for recurring words that give solid clues to the structure of the text.

5. Identify key words in the passage, again particularly words or phrases that are repeated and have theological significance, and do a word study on these to determine their precise meaning. Is the repetition verbatim or does it vary? What is the significance of this?

6. Check the critical apparatus of the original text in a good study Bible to see what problems exist within the text, for instance, what word variations other ancient manuscripts might use.

7. Using literary criticism, do a literary and rhetorical analysis of the text using interior evidence. This includes asking: What is the form of the text (is it an epic, a letter, a hymn, a benediction, a lament, an argument, a story)? In what style is it written? What are its parts? How does each part relate to the whole? How does its form relate to its function? What is the text trying to accomplish rhetorically? What difference is made to the book if this passage is left out? Who are the main characters in the text? What is the conflict? What do they do (i.e., what is the plot)? What is the resolution? How does the thought or action in the text connect with the passages that went before and go after? Who is in power? Who are the primary and secondary characters and what might this suggest? Who is excluded from power? Is there a difference in the way

men and women or rich and poor are treated? Are their words given equal weight? What patterns in action, thought, or expression emerge? What links does this text suggest with other Bible passages? What does not fit or is a puzzle?

8. Sketch the structure or flow of the argument or story so as to understand it better.

9. Consult various resources like Bible commentaries, dictionaries, and atlases to determine, as much as possible, the historical life situation of the text, or its *Sitz im Leben,* and its history of transmission. Determine from your research if your text has been edited and what purposes the editing served. Discover what others say about the passage. To whom or what situation was the text addressed as we have it?

10. State the meaning of the passage in a sentence, if possible. Offer an interpretation only after all of the evidence is carefully analyzed and synthesized.

By listening in this manner, we allow ourselves to be led as much as possible by the biblical text to an understanding of it. Of course, the process is never as linear as this. Arrival at a text's meaning is a process of conversation with it, listening to it in a humble and receptive fashion, yet listening also to the self as a real participant in the relationship. As interpreters, although we try to be as neutral as possible, we nonetheless come to a biblical text with preconceived ideas about it, which Rudolf Bultmann calls our pre-understandings. We try to minimize their influence, yet to some degree they continue to affect our engagement of the text. We make guesses about meaning throughout the process, and we simply withhold final interpretation until the end. Our final interpretation is what our ancestors called the literal sense of the text, or what we call its meaning, without understanding this to be the only interpretation possible. At some point preachers allow themselves to engage the text from the perspective of faith. In this latter exercise they both challenge and are challenged by the text, and by this process they are led to faithful proclamation.

Practical Considerations

One problem with this model for preaching is that the faith dimension of it is largely omitted, unaddressed in Bible class and often in biblical commentaries as though engagement of the text by a believer is necessarily a private or personal task. Some scholars may not articulate theological strategies with the text because they feel that such comments lie outside their own academic discipline or area of competence. Others venture sporadically into theological matters almost as an aside, as though they have two personalities or one hand that does not know what the other is doing. The lack of integration of theology and biblical studies is not new; scholars have known of this problem for some time, and some, like Walter Brueggemann, address it. Also, some biblical commentaries try to speak to the needs of the pulpit and often address matters of faith, for example, *The New Interpreters Bible* and *Interpretation.* Even here the process can be uneven, and theological criticism, at times, can seem hit and miss. Perhaps it is because commentators have not been trained in theological criticism; or they do not agree on what constitutes a theological approach; or they are not sure how best to interpret Scripture for the church. How people in one discipline solve a problem need not be how people in another solve it, for they speak with different goals in mind and often read the Bible with different lenses. Even particular fields have widely differing opinions. Overall, the process of theological engagement of texts remains a neglected topic, and the problem remains acute, as is seen, for example, in the theme of recent books like *Reclaiming the Bible for the Church*[16] and *The Theological Interpretation of Scripture.*[17]

Theological criticism poses a particular problem for scholars who think of biblical studies as religious studies or who trained in the former "objective" model of historical criticism and remain largely unaffected by more contemporary approaches to interpretation. Many of these scholars seem unable or unsure how to claim divine inspiration of the Bible and tend to focus, instead, on the human elements that contribute to biblical form and content. Others may focus on God seen through the human lenses of the text at hand yet avoid claims about the triune God affirmed through broader readings of Scripture. Even classrooms that are open to reading the Bible with new lenses like rhetoric, race, gender, and economics, nonetheless can still avoid engaging the texts for what they say about God, faith, and doctrine. As a result, students can receive the message that the exegetical process they learn is largely sufficient to equip them for the pulpit. Preachers similarly have not been taught to question whether the literal sense that emerges at the end of historical-critical and literary exegesis is adequate for the pulpit. Given this situation, it is not surprising that many sermons across denominational lines focus on what humans should do and omit consideration of God.[18] Typically, preachers who have this failing are unaware of it and do not stop to ensure that, out of their biblical texts, they make claims about who God is, or what God has done, is doing, and has promised to do. This frequent failure is naturally a motive behind this current project.

Preaching normally requires that the preacher say what the text or the sermon is about in one sentence, yet this needs some qualification. Obviously, some ideas are more central to a biblical text than others and some are better than others for preaching. In addition, some texts present more than one idea, or focus, for preaching. Until H. Grady Davis's *Design for Preaching* (Fortress Press, 1958) and Fred B. Craddock's *As One Without Authority* (Abingdon Press, 1971), preachers commonly assumed that a text could be summarized by a propositional statement that could then be expounded in the sermon. That earlier process essentially flattened the biblical text by reducing it to one idea that represented the whole. Nowadays, we understand that the selected idea is not the text in a nutshell but is rather one significant idea in the arena of authentic meaning of a text, without at the same time, being a fully adequate statement in and of itself.

Geography, Setting, and Historical Imagination

The exegetical process outlined in the last section is fairly typical. One way to consider it is to inquire what questions are not asked. Two areas of vital interest to the pulpit are commonly not mentioned in overviews of historical-critical method. The first is geography and the second is God; we examine each in turn. Concerning the first, historical criticism does not exclude geography and setting from consideration, and when a text mentions a place, responsible exegesis dictates that the significance of the place be determined. Not all biblical texts mention geography, however. Still, to assemble any historical analysis historical imagination is needed, and to communicate well in a sermon, it is essential. In sermons, biblical texts must be brought to life, and one way of doing that is to present the biblical material in a real setting with real people dealing with real issues. The setting of a Gospel passage may not be identified in the particular set of verses under consideration; one may have to go back a chapter to discover it. In an epistle it can be the place and circumstances in which it is being written or the place to which it is addressed or in which it is read aloud as part of the ancient worship gathering. Often one cannot be certain and must follow the best guess of the biblical scholars in this regard.

Geography and setting is of central concern in every sermon simply because geography helps make things real and vital, and until a congregation is able to picture a setting in their minds, communication of anything happening in that setting is largely wasted. In a sermon, location is the first information the congregation requires every time there is a change of scenery. Bible atlases and photographic resources can greatly help the preacher to picture a particular geographical setting.

The larger issue here is the use of historical imagination with historical criticism. Sound, not the page, is the true medium of the sermon and everything must be communicated at the time the sermon is delivered. A preacher can be accurate concerning historical assessment and still be boring, unable to communicate the fruits of learning. People generally remember best what they are able to visualize. Unfortunately most of a preacher's education for ministry is focused on the page, not on composing for oral delivery. One means of imagining of this shift to language for auditory comprehension is to conceive of sermon composition not as writing an essay but as making a movie.[19] Preachers commonly have difficulty doing this particularly with the epistles. Here is my own attempt to make a passage from Romans 8:15-25 come alive using geographical and other exegetical information to enliven historical imagination:

> Our passage from Paul's Letter to the Romans is one of the noisiest passages in the entire New Testament. Christians are crying in their suffering, "Abba! Father!" "[All] creation," Paul says, "has been groaning in labor pains until now." "We ourselves," he adds, "groan

inwardly" while we wait for our final salvation and the redemption of our bodies. And even the Holy Spirit, praying to God on behalf of the church, intercedes "with sighs too deep for words." The Greek verb *stenazo*, means sigh or groan, "with [groans] too deep for words." Even the Holy Spirit groans for the church, yearns for the fulfillment of God's purposes.

Why Paul's emphasis on groans? Paul is writing to the church in Rome from his winter shelter in Corinth, Greece, in A.D. 56, and groans are on his mind. Perhaps his wooden roof is groaning under the weight of ice from freezing rain. He may even hear a woman in the next cottage groaning in childbirth: "All creation has been groaning in labor pains until now," he writes. Perhaps he recalls his own groans from past journeys: As he says elsewhere, five times he has been flogged forty lashes minus one; three times beaten with rods; once he received a stoning; often he has been left near death; and many times he has been without food, shelter, and clothing (2 Cor. 11:23-29). Perhaps he even groans out loud as he dictates his letter to Tertius, his secretary who sits by the flickering candle in the drafty room recording his words, for this much we do know: Paul is in agony concerning the divisions in the church. Has he not just patched up divisions in his church in Corinth (2 Cor. 1:23)? When spring comes, and it is again safe for sails on the Mediterranean to be billowing with winds from Africa, he must ship east to Jerusalem to prevent a division. He has collected money from his Greek churches for the poor in the Jerusalem church. Some people in Jerusalem have said that Paul's churches in Ephesus, Corinth, and Galatia are renegade. Paul groans at the possibility that the church of Christ could be divided. After Jerusalem, Paul will sail to seven hills of Rome to deal with division there. In A.D. 49, Emperor Claudius exiled Jewish Christians. Now that Claudius is dead, the exiles have returned home to their old churches after six years, but then, as they are now, old members and new members were a source of conflict.

Everything Paul preaches stands for the unity of the body of Christ.

An important guide for using historical imagination is to picture places, people, and things using descriptive detail that is sparse yet sufficient to make events sound and seem as if they could have just happened. Avoid, as much as possible, going into people's minds, dreams, and feelings, unless these can be communicated to a camera through actions and words of the characters themselves, for what goes on in the interior landscape of the mind is inherently less interesting to listeners.

The Question of Theology

Questions about God are also not normally given special attention in outlining exegetical method, and God is not discussed unless God is specifically mentioned in a text. In such cases comments generally are restricted to what the person in the text thinks about God. Historical-critical exegesis, per se, typically excludes faith-claims, such as may be found in theology, about who God is revealed to be and how life is to be lived before God, yet these are essential matters for the pulpit. They need to be incorporated as part of a preacher's Bible study because these meanings reside within the text taken as Scripture. Some scholars are attentive to this, as we note, as are many preachers, perhaps intuitively. Others might assume that the Bible is already about these subjects and that they are dealt with as a matter of course in answering the rigorous exegetical questions. Many texts do deal with these matters, yet for those that do not, the exegetical process we have outlined will not yield the necessary results. The lenses we bring to a text help determine what we find in it: We bring historical lenses to find history, and we bring theological and homiletical lenses to find faith and affirm relevance.

Interpretation is a fluid process that does not stop once exegesis is complete, although we may think that homiletics takes over at this point. Interpretation continues well beyond historical-critical and literary exegesis and continues even into the pulpit on Sunday, where new insights may still occur and when matters of oral delivery and emphasis shade meaning. Until an interpretation is stated and developed in a fixed written form, at least in the preaching moment itself, effectively there is no interpretation. Homiletics has biblical interpretation at its heart from beginning to end.

Questions of how to preach a text are separate from historical-critical exegesis, yet they are not as removed as we might think, for preachers are always projecting analogies between the biblical text and today that affect what they find in a text. In other words, they are always thinking of theological implications for what history and literary analysis offers. Friedrich Schleiermacher pictured the interpretative path as a hermeneutical "circle" or spiral that goes round and round between then and now as the interpreter gradually assembles an appropriate understanding. Even this image is too orderly for the process most of us observe. We need to add countless random sparks that jump across the diameter and also to relevant materials outside of the text. Finally, at the end of historical-critical exegesis we do not commonly have an interpretation that will effectively preach. We have one essential understanding of the literal sense as history. The theological and homiletical dimensions are still missing.

In this chapter we explored some common ideas that cause difficulty concerning the idea of the literal sense and preaching, and we reviewed the connection of the literal sense to exegesis. We note the kind of information that exegesis excels at providing even as we note its weakness. To understand what is missing by way of theology, the next chapter traces the story of how theological understanding of the literal sense is dominant until after the Reformation and then is largely lost with the Enlightenment and the rise of various kinds of biblical and literary criticism. The final two chapters that conclude this section explore (1) recovering God for the literal sense and (2) theological exegesis to determine a God sense that will preach today.

CHAPTER THREE

A Brief History
of the Literal Sense

What difference does it make if preachers conceive of a literal sense of Scripture? The term itself is less crucial than the issues it represents, for nearly everything about preaching is at stake. If there are no plain meanings of Scripture (allowing for an arena of valid interpretation as opposed to a single meaning), then the Bible cannot function as the normative book upon which the church bases its faith and action. Moreover, if the Bible means anything we make it mean, it can no longer be said to be Scripture, to bear revelation, or to be the Word of God. Proclamation loses its authority. Our early church and medieval predecessors understood this, and they tried to establish the "plain sense" (*sensus literalis*) of Scripture "as its principal meaning, and to give it a theologically normative role in the formation of Christian theology."[1] The reformers actually achieved this goal by naming the literal sense as the only sense of Scripture for purposes of developing doctrine and practice. Their period is one of the last in which the literal sense of the Bible is universally assumed to be theological, that is, having to do with God and faith.

Because we often dismiss biblical criticism prior to the Reformation, we do not pay sufficient attention to the ingenious solution our ancient ancestors found for the problem—a solution that can work for us as well. They conceived of a double-literal sense, a lower one that has to do with history, and a higher one that has to do with God and theology. The reformers later adopted this solution, which complements their recognition of the Bible as both a human document and an instrument of God.

The problem of the literal sense largely was resolved with the reformers. However, beginning with the Enlightenment, the problem returned. No sooner did the reformers put allegory in its place, no sooner did they identify the divine meaning as the literal sense, than modern history emerged to say "I am what the Bible is about," in other words, "This is the literal sense." The problem was compounded because later historical critics assumed that this is what Luther and Calvin intended when they gave primacy to the literal sense. So, once again the church faced the same problem it faced for its first fifteen hundred years: How can it accommodate historical understanding with divine revelation? How can it establish meanings of the Bible that allow it to be Scripture? How can preachers claim with confidence, "This is the Word of God"?

The reformers' solution did not survive the Enlightenment. Eventually, somewhere along the way, God's action throughout history, and in speaking the text, became less central to critical study. Historical-critical scholars became less comfortable speaking of revelation or of the Bible as the inspired Word of God. Preachers often had no training to distinguish those scholars from others who were committed to Bible for the church, no way to differentiate historical commentary from theological. Thus, in our own time, while the Bible is largely recovered for the pulpit in many denominations through use of the lectionary, it is often read with the lens of history, or some of the new lenses of literary criticism, at the expense of theology.

To understand what is lost concerning the literal sense, in the midst of all of this historical and literary gain, we need to consider the "literal" before and after the Reformation. Our preaching forebears show the direction we need to follow.

The Literal Sense Up to the Reformation

The literal sense of Scripture up to the time of Luther and Calvin is fairly consistent, although Origen and Augustine represent two contrasting choices. Origen (A.D. 185–254) holds to the literal sense of passages when it makes sense and obviously relates to faith. In fact, Origen prefers spiritual meanings over the literal and considers them to be higher. He takes as his warrant phrases like 1 Corinthians 2:7: "[W]e speak God's wisdom, secret and hidden, which God decreed before the ages for our glory."[2] Where possible, he preserves the historical events to which the literal sense points, although many texts have no literal sense, for they are untrue or unbelievable as history.[3] He offers many examples, including: a first, second, and third day without sun, moon, stars, or heaven (Genesis 1); casting out uncircumcised children from the people after the eighth day (Gen. 17:14); and sitting for the entire sabbath (Exod. 16:29). Similarly, Origen finds no literal sense in Jesus' command to pluck out only one eye when, in fact, both have sinned (Matt. 5:28-29).[4] Concerning Matthew 10:10, Origen says, "[H]ow would it be possible, especially in those countries where the bitterness of winter is accentuated by icy frosts, to observe the precept that a man should not possess two coats, nor any shoes?"[5] Such texts are intended to communicate a spiritual meaning.

Augustine (354–430), by contrast and following Irenaeus, shows clear preference for the literal, and argues that every text does have a literal meaning. In order to make this claim, he expands the meaning of literal—scholars say he has two levels of literal.[6] In *On Christian Doctrine,* the meaning of a biblical text is its literal meaning if it is edifying in itself.[7] Any text dealing with "faith, the mores of living, and . . . hope and charity" (2:IX) is to be read literally. Only literal texts, about which there can be no ambiguity, can be the basis for arguments concerning doctrine and faith. Obscure passages can be illuminated by clear ones (2:IX). Irenaeus's rule of faith guides interpretation: texts mean what the church says they mean. Interpretation of figurative texts is governed by the rule of love, that is, they must be afforded "an interpretation contributing to the reign of charity" (3:XV). No Bible passage can yield mere commonplace meanings. If a text is unclear or unedifying at face value, Augustine treats it as a figure of speech and in such cases the figurative meaning is part of the literal sense.

The Old Testament poses a particular problem in the early church because history as we know it is not conceived, and understanding of previous times is limited. Our ancestors understood the Bible to belong to a time and culture that was lost and largely irrelevant. Thus, the literal sense was not the most immediate. Godfrey of St. Victor refers to it as the far shore of the river of interpretation: "History is more a shaper of the rituals of the Old Testament, / And on this account is more oriented to the other shore."[8] The near shore for him and others was what God was saying now. Our historical criticism, by striking contrast, gives primacy in the biblical documents to the past as opposed to the present.

For our ancestors, revelation was encoded in the words of the page. Behind the text in the historical events, little or nothing could be discovered because they did not have the tools of modern history. Everything important is contained in God's dictation, and this is the message that God wants people to receive. To toss out the Old Testament, as Marcion does, erases the story of revelation and implies that the Old Testament has a different God. History is nonetheless a constant problem in accepting the literal sense as normative. What does it mean?

Augustine fights to preserve the literal sense of Scripture. Many in his time claim that Noah's ark cannot be literal because Noah could not have caught all species of insects. Augustine responds that they are right, Noah did not catch them, God sent them to the ark: "They shall come in to you" (Gen. 6:20). Concerning "They shall be male and female," he observes that flies occur spontaneously from "corruption"; that bees "have no sex," thus they are not there; and mules are a sterile, hybrid species, "Yet, if it was necessary for the completeness of the mystery, they were there; for even this species has 'male and female.' "[9]

Augustine wrote *The Harmony of the Gospels* to defend the trustworthiness of the "literal." His general defense is that the writers who have not reproduced the self-same form of speech have still reproduced the identical sense intended to be conveyed.[10] Concerning whether the temptation of Jesus took place before or after he was taken to the Temple, Augustine says, "It is, however, a matter of no real consequence, provided it be clear that all these incidents did take place."[11] Concerning Luke's placement of John's imprisonment at the time of Jesus' birth, "we are to understand him [Luke] to have acted by anticipation here, and to have taken the opportunity of recording at this point an event which took place actually a considerable period later."[12] Concerning different versions of the miracle of five loaves, "The truth is, that the one has reported simply a part, and the other given the whole."[13]

When Augustine preached, however, he commonly resorted to allegory because he pursued some God-intended meaning other than mere history. In "The Ten Virgins" (Matt. 25:1-13), the wise bridesmaids carry love as the oil in their lamps, and the foolish bridesmaids carry the oil of pride and flattery.[14] After receiving "the praises of men. . . . they arose, in the resurrection from the dead, they began to trim their lamps, that is, began to prepare to render unto God an account of their works."[15]

Seen against the backdrop of puzzling historical details that seem to await allegorical or theological enrichment, it is surprising that Augustine and those who followed him not only valued the literal sense but gave it primacy. However, by this they mean that (a) it must first be understood before a spiritual or fuller interpretation can be ventured and (b) the Holy Spirit uses it to give the fuller meaning. The literal is not the only sense of Noah: "For what right-minded man will contend that books so religiously preserved during thousands of years, and transmitted by so orderly a succession, were written without an object, or that only the bare historical facts are to be considered when we read them?"[16]

What we see in Augustine is what Nicholas of Lyra later calls a "double-literal" sense. The literal is normative only by extending it to include a theological understanding beyond the grammatical-historical sense of the text. James Samuel Preus provides the most extensive study of the double-literal sense; he calls this second literal sense the "normative-literal" meaning of a text in that it leads to right faith and action.[17] In other words, it is what the church normally recognizes as a text's meaning when a puzzling text functions as Scripture.

We ought not to be surprised at the appearance of a double-literal sense in Augustine or at its continuance through to the Reformation. It arises mainly in relation to the Old Testament and the struggle with whether Hebrew Scripture has integrity on its own or is merely a foreshadowing of truth that is spoken more clearly in the New Testament. For our ancient ancestors, the Old Testament was prophetic of the New Testament that fulfilled it; the New Testament is the Old Testament in clearer expression; the New Testament is "literal sense" of the Old Testament made plain.[18]

By the late–medieval age, the literal sense seemed to be like a wet woolen sweater, stretched and pulled such that its shape seemed to lack definition; yet the idea of two literal senses remained. For Hugh of St. Victor (1096–1141) and those like him, the higher literal meaning arises from the history and cannot contradict it. He instructs his students to use historical chronicles and maps and to memorize the people and events in Genesis, Exodus, Joshua, Judges, Kings, Chronicles, the Gospels, and Acts: "Do not despise these lesser things. They who despise the lesser things gradually fail. . . . I know there are some who want to philosophise immediately. . . . Do not imitate such men."[19] He expands the literal sense to include whatever the biblical writer intends to say: "For this reason it is necessary both that we follow the letter in such a way as not to prefer our own sense to the divine authors, and that we do not follow it in such a way as to deny that the entire pronouncement of truth is rendered in it."[20]

Our purpose is to indicate the presence of a double-literal sense throughout this period. Thomas Aquinas (ca. 1225–1274), whom scholars commonly identify as a champion of historical exegesis in the late–Middle Ages,[21] is nonetheless a product of his time. On one hand the literal "words signify things," that is, historical events. Aquinas adds, "[W]hat is special here [in the Bible] is that the things meant by the words [i.e., the events] also themselves mean something . . . the spiritual sense."[22] He then stretches the literal sense to include the spiritual meanings that the Divine Author intends to say concerning salvation: "[T]he literal sense is that which the author intends, and the author of holy Scripture is God who comprehends everything all at once in his understanding."[23]

Others embraced the double-literal sense. Nicholas of Lyra (ca. 1270–1349) claims it is "just as literal as the first."[24] He claims that the words of the prophet to David are in fact about Christ: "I will be his father, and he shall be my son. When he commits iniquity, I will chasten him with the rod of men, with the stripes of the sons of men" (2 Sam. 7:14). Christ is the real meaning of the Old Testament, hidden to previous generations, and only the church is able to uncover its true literal meaning. As one commentator says, "[E]ven late medieval exegesis maintained that the literal sense served only to illuminate the real aim of the text, which was knowledge about God."[25]

The Literal Sense of the Reformation

The reformers embraced the literal sense as the only meaning of Scripture, yet they too embraced a double-literal sense. The literal for them opposed the interpretations of the majesterium of the Roman church that were without foundation and were used to support it. Martin Luther (1483–1546) does little in his early career to alter the interpretative tradition he receives. Like his peers, he initially understands biblical events to have less connection to the biblical times than to God's plans in the present. Luther reaches a turning point when he recognizes that people in the Old Testament are like people in his own time—engaged in a faith journey in which they have legitimate hope for salvation. Increasingly, he abandons allegory. Revelation becomes located not just in the text but in the history behind the text as well. The grammatical or historical meaning of a text (the first literal level) for him is important: "For even if no one knew that Aaron is a type of Christ, it would not matter, neither can it be proven. We must let Aaron be simply Aaron in the ordinary [i.e., literal] sense, except where the Spirit Himself gives a new interpretation, which is then a new literal sense, as St. Paul, for instance, in the Epistle to the Hebrews makes Aaron to be Christ."[26] Here we see Luther's double-literal sense that allows him to claim only one sense of Scripture: "although the things described in the Scriptures have a further significance, the Scriptures do not on that account have a twofold sense [i.e., literal and spiritual], but only the one which the words give."[27] He adds, "The Holy Spirit is the plainest writer and speaker in heaven and earth, and therefore His words cannot have more than one, and that the very simplest, sense, which we call the literal, ordinary, natural, sense."[28] His second literal sense concerns Christ (*de Christo*), for Scripture is written by God and therefore is about God. All Scripture has a christological meaning: He pictures Christ as the babe in the manger and Scripture as the manger that supports him.[29] One commentator notes, "When Luther spoke of Christ he used the word in a general sense for whatever in the Bible met his need of salvation and forgiveness."[30] The Word of God is the message of salvation speaking through the Scripture and is discerned more readily in some parts of the Bible than others. His literal sense of the Old Testament includes the New Testament as its fulfillment.[31] Since everyone should be able to read Scripture with the benefit of the plain sense—or common sense—this literal "Christ" sense is the common meaning of Scripture.

John Calvin (1509–1564) interprets Scripture from a different theological position rooted in the utter Holiness and sovereignty of a merciful God. Like Luther, he understands the Bible to be an uneven mixture of human document and Divine instrument.

Biblical words transcribed by humans are subject to human limitation. God speaks Scripture.[32] As humans read and interpret these
words accompanied by the Holy Spirit, they receive the message of
salvation as inspired. Calvin values the humanist objective ideal,
yet for him the objective literal reading of Scripture is the true
meaning the Holy Spirit provides: "those whom the Holy Spirit has
inwardly taught truly rest upon Scripture, and that Scripture
indeed is self-authenticated; hence, it is not right to subject it to
proof and reasoning. And the certainty it deserves with us, it
attains by the testimony of the Spirit."[33] When he seeks the "plain
sense" illuminated spiritually, he alludes to his own double-literal
sense. He cites the Road to Emmaus in Luke 24—until Christ opens
the minds and hearts of the disciples, they cannot understand
Scripture. The reader must meet the Holy Spirit with a willing
mind and heart in order to discern God's Word. Soon, many biblical commentators will see such views as unwarranted piety, and
they will close the doors of the literal text to them. One scholar
notes that "much, if not most, of what seems to modern eyes like
eisegesis in Calvin's interpretation of Scripture, is in fact borrowed
from the exegetical tradition. Calvin almost never invents anything
new, although he uses tradition selectively."[34] While his exegesis
informs his theology, "More often, perhaps, theology molded [his]
exegesis."[35]

Augustine articulates many of the exegetical principles that are
later adopted and developed by the reformers, yet their
approaches differ remarkably. For example, the title of Psalm 3
reads, "The Psalm of David when he fled from the face of his son
Absalom." Augustine reads this at a nonhistorical level, based on
verse 3:6 ("'I have fallen asleep and have taken my rest, and I have
risen up, because the Lord will uphold me'") that signals it is about
Christ, and Christ is speaking it.[36] Augustine's primary interest is
Absalom's betrayal of his father as a type or figure of Judas's
betrayal of Jesus. The literal sense functions mostly at the theological level of Christ and Judas.

For Calvin on Psalm 3, by contrast, the grammatical and historical level of the text dominates, or at least how his age imagines history from the chronicles of David's life. He is now an example for
Christian life. Calvin anticipates something like historical criticism
in determining the geographical location of the ark in David's time.

Only at the end of his comments on verse 4, after the historical sense is secure, does he make a link to the life of Christ: "In our day, since there is fulfilled in Christ what was formerly shadowed forth by the figures of the law, a much easier way of approach to God [than David's approach to the ark] is opened up for us, provided we do not knowingly and willingly wander from the way."[37] He does not develop this meaning; instead, he is content with a comparison between how David sought to be close to God and how Christians through Christ can be close to God.

Augustine and Calvin live at opposite ends of the era of Christian double-literal interpretation. By Calvin's time, the Old Testament is no longer assumed to be simply about Christ. Still, the advent of modern biblical criticism is much needed: Scholars claim that Moses is the human author of the Pentateuch simply on the basis of a literal reading of Jesus' words in Mark 7:10, "For Moses said, 'Honor your father and your mother.'"[38] As long as the Old and New Testaments are understood to be a theological unity, the New is the standard whereby critical decisions are made concerning the Old, and scholarly exploration of diversity in the Bible and distinct historical foundations is limited.

Since fourfold exegesis was no longer the basis of biblical study, other approaches were needed to replace it. Philipp Melanchthon (1497–1560) provided one alternative with his *loci communes* or common "places," "locations," or "topics." Suggested in part by classical rhetoric, these *loci* were categories of thought he found in Scripture that the church traditionally relied upon, discussed, reformulated, and clarified—they were key doctrines. Common places provided lenses with which preachers could read texts and understand their meaning with greater clarity. Some Lutheran books on systematic theology still use the term *loci communes* to organize their material. Carl E. Braaten and Robert W. Jenson include the following *loci* in their *Christian Dogmatics*: the triune God, the knowledge of God, the creation, sin and evil, the person of Jesus Christ, the work of Christ, the Holy Spirit, the church, the means of grace, Christian life, and eschatology. The authors explain their approach:

> A *locus* in this sense is a point at which the historic teachings and theological investigations of the church are brought into focus. Each *locus* is developed on its own terms, without deduction from

the others; and that is what mandates this more ancient method for us. . . .

. . . [T]he *loci* mark the centers around which the church has in fact been compelled to gather its reflections. Any actual set of dogmatic *loci* is, of course, a proposal by the author or authors about the exact location of these centers.[39]

Common places are also at the heart of Melanchthon's homiletic (though he himself is not permitted to preach), for they provide a means for preachers to link scriptural texts. He provides a basis for the doctrinal sermon that continues to the present: a preacher finds a doctrine in Scripture and then develops it, freely visiting other texts along the preaching route as a means of gathering further insights. This approach was recently challenged by Hans Frei and others who argue that Scripture cannot be boiled down and reduced to propositions without loss of meaning. As one scholar puts it, Melanchthon's *loci* "meant that every great text had a main point, idea, theme or thesis (*argumentum, status,* or *scopos dicendi*) to which everything was logically related and toward which everything moved."[40] His approach has ambiguous implications, for preachers will take nearly the next five hundred years to recognize that a text may have many different ideas that express its theme; that logic is not the only principle of textual coherence; and that sermons need not have a set number of points to address a theme.

Matthias Flacius Illyricus (1520–1575), credited with writing the first textbook on hermeneutics, provides a second alternative to fourfold exegesis. He extends the literal sense of a text to "the sense that it conveyed to its original readers."[41] He builds on the work of Melanchthon and others. His simple approach to exegesis is summarized as follows: "(1) a general orientation that focuses on the triune God and God's work; (2) a broad knowledge of the fundamental topics and concerns of Scripture; (3) the use of linguistic helps; (4) perseverance in meditation and study of the text; (5) passionate prayer; (6) Christian experience in daily life; (7) a comparison of parallel passages in Scripture; and (8) the use of good translations and faithful exegetes."[42] A scientific approach to biblical studies begins to emerge in Illyricus's method, but as important for our purposes is the faith stance of the interpreter that he encourages in most of his steps. This commitment to faith and theology is a part of reading Scripture and is an essential characteristic of the Reformation. Contemporary scholars who discuss this feature of Reformation hermeneutics often seem to lament it as an unfortunate remnant of the medieval age that the reformers gladly would abandon if they knew better. These scholars suggest that Luther and Calvin are right when they affirm the literal sense as the only sense of Scripture, and Calvin is right when he admires the humanist ideal of an objective, scientific approach to interpretation, but they would ditch their theological readings. A more positive attitude is possible: The reformers say that Scripture is the church's book, and they cannot conceive of it being read in a manner that strips it of its God-centered meaning as God's Word spoken both "then" and "now." Scripture and God sense go hand in hand.

Post-Reformation Criticism: The Death of the Theological Literal Sense

The Enlightenment represents a major shift in human thought. People to this time conceived of the universe in terms of divine will, natural order, and events unfolding largely according to God's plan. Knowledge was fixed and given. Now, with the recovery of Aristotle's emphasis on reason, they conceive of reason independent of nature and of knowledge arising out of experience. When a major shift of paradigm occurs (of the sort our post-Enlightenment contemporary world has experienced moving from the modern to the postmodern), the new is not entirely new. Elements of it are embedded and unnoticed in the old. When these elements come to the fore, what is dominant recedes and what is unaccented becomes highlighted, rather like what happens when a negative of a photograph is developed and shadows become light. In this case, as the influence of theology recedes, science comes to the fore.

Five implications of this follow for the literal sense of Scripture and for preaching: First, the human elements of the text gradually become the focus of meaning in the text, and theological meaning becomes secondary. Second, natural explanations of events including miracles tend to be sought over supernatural. Third, the interpretative focus shifts from the biblical text itself to the vast uncharted historical events and territory behind the biblical texts. Fourth, the authority of the Bible is questioned in new ways:

History offers competing claims for the literal sense. As a result, the ability of Scripture to govern faith and morals for the church is undermined. New ways are sought to shore it up. Fifth, the grammatical and historical senses become distinguished from each other as historical method gains hold; already by the early 1700s Augustin Calmet, in the first dictionary of the Bible, speaks of "le sens grammatical," which implies a literal reading of what the text says, and "le sens littéral et historique," which provides what it means.[43] This historical sense of Scripture eventually becomes confused with the single meaning of Scripture to which the reformers refer.

Some scholars like Richard A. Muller are openly critical of developments that occur after 1600:

- the primary intention of the text is no longer "to offer a divinely inspired message to the ongoing community of faith" and becomes "to recount the sentiments of the dead"
- the meaning of a biblical text is not found "[in] the scope and goal of the canonical revelation of God" but is now located in "a hypothetically isolatable unit of text that has its own *Sitz im Leben* [situation in life] distinct from surrounding texts or from the biblical book in which it is lodged"
- the primary locus of interpretation moves from the church in conversation with its exegetical tradition to "scholarly encounter in the confines of an academic study."[44]

Nonetheless, preachers can celebrate the gains of historical criticism. We have things to say about the texts and their backgrounds that our ancestors did not know, and we have answers to many questions that simply puzzled them. Nearly every approaching Enlightenment development in biblical and literary studies will have some impact on the literal sense because it is the only sense. For example, the question of who writes a book of the Bible is central to the literal sense only if it is linked to what the human author intends. For many years, scholars have conceived of Isaiah as the product of three authors. Today, authorial questions—and hence the text's meaning—now tend to be handled in light of the argument of an entire book. Gerald T. Sheppard dismisses the standard notions of First, Second, and Third Isaiah and replaces them with a notion of a unified witness, an approach that will generate new textual meanings.[45]

As a further example of the impact of historical studies on the literal sense, throughout much of the nineteenth and twentieth centuries scholars connected the meaning of Scripture with the earliest historical material, namely the original text, the original form of the text, and the original intention of the human author or editor. Knowledge improved about the texts and their traditions. As a negative side effect, however, preachers tended to devalue the literal text and place higher value on earliest layers of the textual tradition instead of staying with the canonical form that was received by the church.

Different kinds of biblical criticism emerged (e.g., historical, source, redaction, form, tradition, sociological) and opened new and enriching dimensions of biblical texts, nearly all of which have to do with their history, origins, purpose, original forms, and social influences. These understandings affected what preachers could say about God in the texts, though these interpretations were not interested in theology, per se. The same can be said for new modes of literary interpretation that allow greater immediate access to biblical texts in the present moment and highlight things not seen in them before (e.g., new criticism, structuralism, deconstruction, rhetorical criticism, reader response, Marxist criticism, feminist/womanist criticism, new historicism). Each builds upon (even as it may reject) types of criticism that precede it as part of an ongoing conversation. Stephen Bonnycastle's *In Search of Authority: An Introductory Guide to Literary Theory* (Broadview Press, 1996) is probably the most accessible literary guide available for those who lack this important background.[46] For most preachers, these approaches serve to open new avenues of textual exploration and clarify differing critical perspectives of biblical commentators. They can also serve to further de-theologize the literal sense because God is not their focus. Of course we need to be cautious in our use of the term "literal sense" in this recent period because we tend to speak instead to the "sense" or "meaning" or "meanings" of a text since we no longer have need to distinguish the literal sense from the other medieval senses.

The Current State of Affairs

The "Enlightenment promise" that scholars might be able to agree on the literal sense of Scripture never materialized and instead, these various kinds of criticism came to function as new lenses with which to see things in the text that were not noticed before. Ironically, the number of candidates for the literal sense increased. The reformers argued that "Scripture interprets Scripture" *(Scriptura Scripturam interpretatur)* and that Scripture is interpreted by Scripture alone *(sola Scriptura)* against Roman claims that the majesterium of the church had the final say in what texts mean. The reformers, nonetheless, brought their own theological interests to the texts along with any resources that could assist them. Following the Enlightenment, this tradition continued. Scripture was interpreted by Scripture, science, history, comparative religion, sociology, anthropology, archaeology, literary studies, and every other tradition that is deemed relevant, both inside the church and outside. The new "meaning(s)" of the text are legitimate and allow preachers to see what the texts actually say. If these approaches are not the literal sense of Scripture as the Word of God, they nonetheless help us discuss the text and to discern that Word. In many pulpits, some of these meanings easily get confused with what preachers need most to focus upon in the texts.

The need for theological approaches to Scripture has been recently highlighted in the work of a number of scholars. Brevard Childs uses historical-critical tools in his canonical criticism and also tries to "work in a theologically responsible exegetical fashion."[47] In fact, he sees his canonical approach not as a method but as a theological perspective. He honors the biblical texts as documents of faith that speak the Word of God and shape faith communities today. He finds inadequate both the liberal embrace of historical criticism at the expense of theology and the conservative attempts to resist historical criticism by theological dogmatism. He avoids imposing theological categories on the text, yet he brings faith into the conversation in determining the text's meaning.[48] He identifies four sets of polarities that are to be maintained as tensions in biblical criticism: (1) between evaluating Israel's history in a neutral manner and treating it as a confessional stance from within the community of faith, (2) between viewing history as human agency and as God's agency, (3) between interpreting Israel's history as though it is the same as every other nation's and objectifying it into a unique story of salvation history, and (4) between recognizing that Israel has tampered with history in putting its perspective forward and valuing what Israel has chosen to emphasize in its history.[49] Childs does not conceive of his approach as a method, yet preachers can benefit even by nurturing these polarities in their sermons such that both historical criticism and theology are honored.

Childs works behind the text in its prehistory and traditions, and in front of it in its history of interpretation and its meaning for the faith community to the present day. He wants to know how the text influences these communities, past and present. He also works with the text giving priority to its final form in the canon of Scripture for the community of faith. For preachers, this perspective is helpful. David L. Bartlett, inspired by Childs, comments, "We [as preachers] want to know what is there in the Gospel of Matthew, not in Q or some source called 'M', or in some pre-Matthean version of the Sermon on the Mount. We do not care much whether an ecclesiastical redactor fiddled with the ending of John's gospel, or the canonical Gospel includes chapter 21, and that needs to be part of our interpretation."[50] While preachers need not restrict their perspective on texts to their final form when Scripture is canonized (the second ending of John 21 may be worth pondering as a second ending), we nonetheless benefit from staying focused on the text as it is received. Earlier traditions or forms do not provide more authentic Christian witness.

Nearly fifty years ago, Raymond Brown tried to accommodate a theological approach as well as a historical approach to Scripture. He talked of three senses of Scripture, the literal, the "typical," and the *Sensus Plenior*, or fuller sense, intended by God.[51] That he is Roman Catholic is significant; for the Roman Church was slow to adopt historical criticism, and he sought to preserve traditional interpretations of biblical texts alongside the new historical readings.

Many biblical scholars take theological turns in their writing. Gail O'Day combines theology and historical criticism in her work.[52] Richard B. Hays identifies four tasks in New Testament ethics, one of which is synthetic. In this, he places the biblical text in its canonical context by utilizing one of three "focal images": community, cross, and new creation.[53] Each of these has the potential not just to illuminate the human tasks of ethical response to the Word but also to make significant claims about God. The synthetic task of ethics is close to homiletics. The difficulty with so many scholars and preachers who do take a theological turn with the Bible is that the focus remains on the human side of the divine-human encounter (this is a particular danger in ethics), which is just what historical criticism does and what so many poor sermons do, instead of focusing on both humanity and God. Plainly, a postmodern age has difficulty speaking boldly of the mighty acts of God.

Walter Brueggemann has the pulpit in mind more than most biblical scholars. He combines historical criticism with theology by asking two basic questions of texts. "We shall be asking, *what* is uttered about God? And this will require us to pay attention to *how* Israel uttered about God."[54] He advocates revised methods of interpretation that do not rely upon outdated positivistic assumptions that meaningful statements can be made only about sensory data and empirical evidence (i.e., excluding faith). He offers three requirements for a new approach to criticism and interpretation: (1) "discern what of the older historical criticism is to be retained and how it is to be used," (2) value sociological and rhetorical approaches that "allow both for the density of social processes coded in the text" along with the proclamatory power of the text ("the generative, constitutive power of the textual utterance"), and (3) reexamine and reorder the old assumption that historical criticism takes the lead and theological interpretation follows afterward.[55]

As preachers, we need all the help we can get in focusing on God in addition to humans in biblical texts. We now turn to how we might helpfully reconceive of the literal sense from a homiletical perspective. For more than two decades, many scholars have been alert to the crisis in historical criticism; yet, change often comes slowly, and many scholars do not recognize the problem. As Carl E. Braaten and Robert W. Jenson recently said, "The methods of critical reason have tended to take over the entire operation of biblical interpretation, marginalizing the faith of the church and dissolving the unity of the Bible as a whole into a multiplicity of unrelated fragments."[56] Faith is seen as something that can only jeopardize a fair reading of the text; Scripture is interpreted to be about human belief and action; scientific method is used to limit what God is able to do; and if God's action can be discerned at all, it is ignored because it comes through the fallible and limited filter of human witnesses. Childs adds, "[T]he paradox of much of Biblical Theology was its attempt to pursue a theological discipline within a framework of Enlightenment's assumptions which necessarily resulted in its frustration and dissolution."[57]

The opinion of theological disciplines other than homiletics on how to recover Scripture as Scripture is important, as are their suggestions as to how to accomplish theological focus. However, homiletics needs to develop its own perspective because its first concern is with preaching. It is fundamentally practical, and it has its own contribution to make to the discussion. We will argue for the need to recover a version of the double-literal sense held by our ancient preaching ancestors.

CHAPTER FOUR
The Literal Sense and God

As preachers we need to recover our own contemporary version of the medieval double-literal sense. We need to affirm, on one hand, what we have learned from historical and literary critical approaches concerning the incredible richness of biblical texts as texts; the new meanings that have not been seen before; the limitations of our own individual perspectives and any interpretative claims we make; and interpretation as a social act that has economic and political implications. On the other hand, we need to put these historical and literary readings in the service of God. We need to claim that theological readings of biblical texts are the only way to claim them as Scripture and that theological meanings depend upon the historical-critical sense and are more significant. Without a double-literal sense, historical criticism becomes the final arbiter on matters of faith. Some preachers try to resolve historical issues, like the original form of a text or what really happened in a miracle, as though in doing so they have resolved what is most important. A double-literal sense brings history and theology into relationship as a team to serve the issues that really matter for preaching.

There is a further practical advantage to recovering a double-literal sense. Preachers need clear ways to conceive and apportion their preparation time. They receive excellent instruction in biblical classes in how to do biblical exegesis and the model they get is thorough, often more thorough than most preachers can execute in the midst of heavy pastoral responsibility. Nonetheless they take that model into the parish and may spend most of the week doing historical and literary analysis of their text (or texts). Their instruction leads them to think that once exegesis is complete, they are like Moses on Mount Nebo—most of the journey to the pulpit is complete and all that remains is a matter of technique and popularizing the message. In fact, historical-critical exegesis on its own only takes preachers to the Red Sea; yet until we have a theological understanding of the text and have discerned where God wants us to go, the waters do not part and our way through the desert is unclear, thus the largest portion of our biblical journey remains up ahead.

Biblical scholars eventually will find better ways to make historical criticism serve Scripture. Even if this happens tomorrow, as preachers, we will continue to make common mistakes: We develop analogies on the basis of historical similarity instead of theology rooted in history. We preach textual images that do not capture theological significance. There is a similar danger in the opposite direction: We are tempted to skip the history and go straight to the textually based theology, as though in doing so, we do not distort it. Unless history and theology are distinct yet parallel tracks of preparation, we lose sight of one or the other. They are independent yet related areas of exploration. Instead of waiting for people in related disciplines to find their own discipline-related solutions, we need to be clear on our own processes to ensure that both history and theology are duly honored from the pulpit.

It is one thing to determine that preachers need a higher theological literal sense, and it is another to agree on what that might be or how it might be achieved. How we read the Bible is not an individual or departmental matter. Ethicists, theologians, preachers, educators, and biblical scholars do not each have their own way of reading the text nor do individuals in the pew. David E. Demson argues from Karl Barth and Hans Frei that how we read Scripture is rooted not in methodology but in inspiration—in our relationship to Jesus Christ through the power of the Holy Spirit. Just as Jesus' disciples were gathered, upheld, and sent, and the resurrection an affirmation of all that he had been for them, so, too, as disciples we are gathered, upheld, and sent by Christ in and through power of the preached Word. "There is a distinction, but no gap, between the text and what it describes in this regard. There is a distinction in that Jesus, and not the text, executes this threefold choosing of many, but there is no gap in that what Jesus does and what the text describes him as doing are one, for Jesus ever utters his own Word as the Word of the appointment, calling, and commissioning of many."[1] In other words, the way we all read Scripture is held together and united in Christ.

One can affirm the unity of Scripture found in Jesus Christ and

58

recognize within that unity much diversity, not least in how the meaning of a biblical text is construed. One can acknowledge that scriptural meaning is not up to individuals or to individual theological disciplines and still affirm that different vantage points afford a unique perspective with which to view a text. Homiletics in particular is important for the conversation for it must provide practical concrete guidance to preachers with congregations in view.

Preaching brings the fruit of a strong historical-critical study of the text forward to the congregation so that they are enabled to hear the text's message afresh for themselves. At the same time, the church studies the Bible as sacred Scripture and listens for the revealed Word of God. Preachers cannot preach effectively until an encounter with that Word has taken place. Traditional understandings of the practice of exegesis might encourage us to believe that with history we are drawing something out from the text and with theology we are reading something into the text. This misimpression needs our immediate attention for when theological questions are not asked, and when the text is not engaged from the perspective of faith, the testimony of the Spirit is hampered.

Being Literal About Exegesis and Eisegesis

The difference between exegesis and eisegesis hinges on the literal sense. These two terms no longer correspond to their literal meanings. Exegesis ("to lead out of") denotes that one is drawing meaning out of the text while eisegesis ("to lead into") denotes bad interpretation, taking meaning into the text that is not there. These terms are convenient, for they suggest a boundary between what is legitimately inside the arena of authentic interpretation and what is not; thus they provide a quick way of teaching an important distinction in scholarly research. The term "eisegesis" has come into frequent use recently with the refinement of historical-critical method and the need to identify improper procedure.

In the early and medieval church, exegesis corresponded to a direct encounter with God's spoken and literal Word. Discerning the literal sense was a matter of grasping the individual words, grammar, and syntax, and relating them to the faith—not primarily to the history, culture, and events behind the text. We might think of their spiritual senses as eisegesis and that this should have been as clear to them as it is to us, yet for our ancestors, the spiritual senses (together with the higher literal sense) were the real meaning. The text for them was always read for connections with the faith, thus for all practical purposes, exegesis was literally "leading out."

The biblical text in a sermon was often just a starting place for a conversation, a location to mine for ideas or doctrines or connections to other texts. They preached the entire Bible and fullness of the gospel as understood and expressed by the church, its Scriptures, its authorities such as the church fathers, and church councils. They expanded a biblical "text" by bringing to it, first, all of their arts and education to determine the historical sense, and second, the faith and doctrines of the church to determine the higher literal sense. Eisegesis, had they used the term, meant reading something into a text that misrepresented either the faith or the intention of the text or its author. Their rules of exegesis were rooted in the grammar and history of the text and the theology of the church. As long as one was "led"—as only the Holy Spirit can lead—to thoughts about the saving acts of Jesus Christ by prompts from the text (in a manner that our age might disparage as free association), then exegesis, not eisegesis, was employed.

The situation is different today. We recognize that neutral or uniform interpretation is impossible, for interpreters always bring their own perspectives to a text, though our age favors history. History allows us to use Scripture in various ways as lenses. One purpose of exegesis is to see history and gain an accurate sense of what happened. Another is to see what the text says: Historical and literary criticism in particular help us to see how rich texts are in meaning. A further purpose is to see ourselves: to use the text to exegete our own lives, to identify our personal and cultural biases, to eliminate those biases that contradict who we are called to be in Christ, and to hear the text afresh in its literary context and historical setting so that it challenges our attitudes and assumptions. A related purpose of exegesis is to see our world and what needs to change. In other words, exegesis includes everything we bring to a text by way of history "behind" it and of our worldview "in front of" it in discerning its meaning. When the term "eisegesis" is used, it tends to be reserved for that which is nonhistorical such as theological, ideological, or impressionistic interpretations.

The biblical text we proclaim is never just the biblical text. Brevard S. Childs draws on Gerhard Ebeling to observe, "[T]he study of the Old and New Testaments as a historical discipline can no longer be limited to the so-called canonical scriptures.... Rather, the use of all historical sources which are pertinent to the subject is required without distinction."[2] Daniel Patte has a different take on the same issue, arguing that it is impossible to read just the text: "Yet I want to go further and claim that any critical exegesis is the interpretation of existing interpretations. This is true even when the critical exegesis presents itself as the interpretation of the text itself (for instance, through the rigorous use of a new critical method)."[3] Our age expands "text" to include history, hermeneutics, and social-scientific disciplines. In using the term "exegesis," "leading out" is commonly also "leading in."

The same is true on a personal level. What we bring to the text is many things—our understanding of language and history, experience of wealth or poverty, consciousness of feminist and other such perspectives, faith in Christ, recent experiences, and so forth. Even though we try to read the text with some degree of neutrality to allow the word we find there to be other than the word we bring to it, exegesis is a process of listening, interacting, receiving, and indwelling the text that is far from objective.[4] For this reason, perhaps we should discard the terms "exegesis" and "eisegesis" as simplistic, belonging to an age that believes that complete objectivity is possible.

The term "exegesis" is deep-rooted in our preaching tradition, however, and serves an essential purpose. Preachers still need to do exegesis and still need to avoid other things. Still, what is exegesis and eisegesis depends on one's perspective. To bring a faith perspective and to employ theological criticism in reading a text might be labeled eisegesis by scholars in universities and also in seminaries. Alternatively, if one takes the position that the Bible is Scripture and needs to be read as such, then exegesis that leaves God out misinterprets the scriptural message. Biblical commentators who are sensitive to this move in and out of theological reflection. In order for preachers to get to God in exegesis, they need to follow a deliberate, extended path of exegesis that we call theological criticism. The purpose, of course, is for God to get to us and for us to hear the text with a willingness to obey God's Word.

Pursuit of a Higher Literal Sense

We need to recover not only some notion of "literal sense" but also the practice of a double-literal sense as a means to resolve the tension between history and theology. The term "literal sense" arises out of (1) the church's agreement to allow the canonical set of books to guide its faith, worship, and daily life, and (2) the ability of Scripture through the Holy Spirit both to bear witness to the One who saves and to carry that transforming message of salvation into the lives of individual members of the congregation. The term "literal sense" is not widely used today for clear reasons: It is easily confused with fundamentalistic or literalistic readings; it can be interpreted to imply that there is a single meaning of a text; and it is less needed because the spiritual senses are dismissed. It is still a useful term for preachers to retain because of its rich role in history and because Reformation tradition (and now Roman as well) affirms the literal sense as the only sense for deciding faith and doctrine. It still carries God's authority, promise, and guarantee.

In claiming the authority of Scripture and the importance of historical-critical methodology in discerning the Word, we affirm with our ancestors that the Bible is:

- the Word of God and an authoritative means whereby God communicates God's will to humans
- the record of God's ongoing relationship with the people of Israel and thus repeatedly demonstrates what humans are called to be and how humans respond to God's will
- the record of how God initiates and responds in relation to us and creation, thereby providing the foundation of our knowledge and experience of God
- the basis of our teachings and doctrines concerning what we are to believe, how we are to live, and what we are to hope
- the story of God's ongoing history of salvation.

We also affirm the authority of the canonical Bible as the standard for faith, worship, and practice. Thus, in pursuing higher literal sense(s) we do not look to areas to which we do not extend authority. We are not claiming the authority of reconstructed pre-history of the Bible, or a reconstructed Q as Scripture or "the fifth gospel"; nor are we claiming the earliest traditions of Scripture as "more Scripture" or "more authentic" than others, for instance the sayings scholars judge to be most authentic of the historical Jesus, the portions of the Bible that most conform to our personal inclinations, or those in which it is easiest to hear God's Word of justice (even though some portions of Scripture are very difficult, if not seemingly impossible, for us). Nor do we claim that authority of Scripture extends to issues such as the Pauline authorship of the Pastorals, for the text that we acknowledge as authoritative is Scripture in its canonical form, and does not include the authors behind the text. Thus, we affirm much about the background or historical origins of the Bible, and we allow it to enhance our understanding of a higher literal sense without altering what is, in fact, Scripture. Discretion is needed, for not everything that lies in or behind the text is of the same value or order of importance and not all passages have equal theological weight.

The Bible as history and Scripture as a sacred text make competing claims for the literal sense. Scholars suggest differing resolutions that can guide formulation of higher literal sense. Barnabas Lindars suggests that historical critics do not have to be as defensive of their turf as they often are: "Most people are alive to the danger of taking a quotation out of context to back up a theological argument without regard to its real meaning. On the other hand the historical critic may well equally miss the real meaning out of concern to delve beneath the text in order to answer questions of historical origins."[5] He argues that critical study of the Bible need not deny the inspired nature of Scripture. However, he implies that miracles can be discarded without damaging the teachings or doctrines in the text, perhaps in the manner of Bultmann's demythologizing.[6] Lindars's literal sense, in fact, may water down the text and leave little room for God to act.

Elisabeth Schüssler Fiorenza some years ago identified future directions for criticism and preaching. She saw danger in the failure of historical criticism to be of relevance for the congregation: "However, the questions explored by historical-literary Biblical scholarship and those raised by believers and churches today are often so disparate that it is often impossible to 'apply' a historical-critical interpretation, addressing questions of scholarship, to a pastoral situation."[7] Her solution is to diminish the text and keep the history behind the text: She wants a "new critical hermeneutics [that] does not center on the text but on the people whose story with God is remembered in the texts of the Bible."[8] Specifically, she seeks an interpretative strategy that will challenge androcentrism. For preaching there is advantage in focusing on people in relationship with God wherever possible, but this approach loses the centrality of the text, at least as Scripture.

James Wm. McClendon, Jr., speaks of a solution that honors the text as Scripture and as history. His solution draws on the communion of saints to fuse the two and make them inseparable.

> *[T]he present Christian community [is] the primitive community and the eschatological community.* In other words, the church now is the primitive church and the church on the day of judgment is the church now; the obedience and liberty of the followers of Jesus of Nazareth is *our* liberty, *our* obedience. This is not meant as a denial of the facts of history.... [R]ather, it is a justification *for* intense biblical study by every intelligible means, since the biblical story has present, not mere antiquarian, relevance.[9]

Sandra M. Schneiders argues for a similar interplay between faith and history. For her, the union of the two is found in the one Jesus of faith who is both historical and actual:

> Obviously the proclaimed Jesus... is both more and less than the historical Jesus.... [M]ore... insofar as the gospels present not only history but the transhistorical, not only facts but theological interpretation of the facts. However, the historical Jesus, precisely because of its rootedness in and relationship to the actual Jesus, creates a critical tension in the proclamation itself that grounds the endless efforts of scholars to interpret the text and of believers to understand it. In this sense, the textual Jesus never exhausts the riches of the One who is mediated by the historical Jesus.[10]

My own solution is to (1) affirm with McClendon and Schneiders the necessary holding together of the historical and theological and (2) accomplish this by recovering from our preaching ancestors a revised double-literal sense of Scripture related to God. History and theology should not be conceived as poles that compete for the literal sense. I give one kind of priority to historical-critical interpretation of texts because without it there can be no reliable theological interpretation, and I give another kind of priority to theological interpretation, reserving it for final arbitration on matters of faith. This is the literal sense most helpful for preachers and the literal sense our Reformation ancestors affirmed when they established the literal sense of the text as our standard. When preachers speak of the literal sense of Scripture it must be to affirm the higher literal sense, the product of theological exegesis rooted in historical-critical inquiry.

The God Sense as the Higher Literal Sense

The words "theocentric" or "Christocentric" are viewed by many biblical critics as bad words when attached to biblical criticism, yet if preachers are not theocentric or Christocentric, they have not done their task. Our higher literal sense needs to be theocentric or Christocentric. David L. Bartlett reminds preachers that "we do not preach so that people may encounter the Bible, but so that people may encounter Christ."[11] Elizabeth Achtemeier is characteristically blunt in her assessment of much preaching: "Because much of the church in this country no longer believes or expects to hear God speaking through its Scriptures, it is therefore not very Christian anymore. And, of course, the results in our mainline churches have been devastating."[12] A recent article claims that Generation X is looking for traditional orthodox expressions of the faith that do not substitute social justice for theology.[13] People now may be looking precisely for God. If this analysis is correct, an important balance needs to be restored between evangelism and social justice that demonstrates willingness to talk about God.

Robert W. Jenson is a theologian who has preaching in focus when he sets out the goal for preachers, derived in part from Irenaeus: "Therefore, among the questions with which we approach any text or set of texts or tradition or redaction...there is one that must always be asked: What does this piece of the Bible tell about the identity of God? Which God is it that Israel and the church worship?"[14]

The relationship of God to Scripture was a common topic throughout the last century, not least for Barth, who asserts the need for the preacher to get out of the way of God speaking, and even Bultmann, who is concerned that Scripture brings listeners to an existential decision for God. In 1974, James M. Gustafson defined Scripture simply as "the revelation of the action of God."[15] He pointed to articles by H. Richard Niebuhr during World War II to argue that the most significant shift in ethics in the mid–twentieth century was "the introduction into ethical thinking of the idea of 'a God who acts,' or a 'God who speaks' in particular historical circumstances. . . . The primary question became not 'how ought we to judge this event?' Nor even 'What ought we to do in this event?' but 'What is God doing in this event? What is he saying to us in this event?' "[16]

Gustafson speaks of ethics, but the central question in determining the higher literal sense(s) for preaching can be the same, *What is God doing in this text?* A related question, *What is God saying in this text?* provides the backbone for early and medieval exegesis. This is a difficult question to address, and frankly, it is much easier to address in an age in which the historical background of the text is irretrievably lost, obscure, or apparently irrelevant, as it seems in early church and medieval times, and when God's revelation is tied to the words and grammar of the text and united with the message of salvation. Still, we learn sufficiently from history that, while Origen can only hear God's voice and can hear no human author speaking, we can listen for both author and Author as legitimate and essential parts of exegesis.

Another vital question for the higher literal sense(s) is, *What is God doing behind this biblical text?* If God in one of the persons of the Trinity is not mentioned within a text, the larger story behind the text needs to be considered: Why was it identified as God's Word and preserved as such? God's identity is disclosed through actions. Questions about God do not normally derive from history, for history is most comfortable with what a person at some time and place might think about God and is mistrustful of the supernatural and of truth claims about God. History nonetheless helps us answer God questions, for we could say very little about what lies behind a text without it.

When we ask *What is God doing in or behind this text?* we do not do so from an objective perspective nor are we open to whatever impressions of the divine we may discover. Rather, we ask it as a church, as people who already know the triune God, and we seek what we may know of this God, not some other. The God who is revealed through Scripture is legitimately sought in Scripture, and the biblical text's answer to *Who is God? What is God saying? What is God doing?* is a way of arriving at a legitimate literal sense, a higher literal sense(s) of the biblical text when it is read as Scripture. Because it invariably centers on God as a person of the Trinity, for simplicity we may call the higher literal sense the God sense.

Many biblical texts, including favorite ones like the prodigal son, do not speak of God directly. When dealing with those texts, we read them in context and in their historical setting. This can lead to reflection concerning God. When we seek God's relationship to textual events and issues, the text does, in fact, give answers, although our training in this regard is so lacking that we may require some practice to discover them. Here we reclaim for preaching the meaning "exegesis" has for most of the life of the church. Exegesis includes the theological criticism to which the biblical text legitimately "leads." This leading is in contrast to wild free-association or to making links that have no logical or historical connection to the text or the church's teachings. Theological leading depends on theological resources and is similar to the historical leading that draws on historical and literary resources outside the text. Both have legitimate claim to the practice known as exegesis.

One can argue something that science recognizes: The questions we ask affect the data we examine. Sarah Smith, a graduate student in homiletics, visited several denominations and discovered that each has its own ways of reading Scripture for purposes of preaching: "Southern Baptists tend to find a message of personal salvation in texts; Mennonites tend to find peacemaking; Roman Catholics tend to find a message for moral living; Episcopalians tend to find the Eucharist; and Methodists tend to find social justice."[17] She used these broad generalizations to illustrate that people come to texts with preconceived ideas of what they will find and where their sermons will go. This unconscious practice can limit our ability to hear what the text is authentically saying, thus the questions we ask a text are important. Questions about God in the text get at the nature of Scripture as the Word of God.

Other disciplines may think that defining a higher literal sense gets dangerously close to a single approach to Scripture. Werner

Jeanrond is passionate about the need for many ways to read the Bible, especially ways that "combine the ancient Christian tradition of a theological reading of the scriptures with the modern and postmodern hermeneutical strategies of retrieval and suspicion."[18] To make precise recommendations for preaching does not go against this openness, nor does it limit other ways in which biblical texts can be read and that are beneficial for preachers to employ. Homiletics nonetheless has a definite goal of a sermon for Sunday for which precise methodological suggestions are needed. These assist preachers in discerning what to focus on in a biblical text for the community of faith and also to know why some sermons are powerful (those that focus on what God can do), others are not (those that never get to God), and still others may seem powerful without good reason (those based solely in rhetoric and charisma).

Several of us in homiletics are attentive to the "God question."[19] The theme sentence of the text (or what I elsewhere call the major concern of the text) is one expression of its God sense and, normally, should have God as its subject. It is short, memorable, uses a single clause, and makes one claim about God as witnessed in or by the biblical text. One sentence cannot fully express a higher literal sense(s) of the text, but in providing a God-centered lens with which to view the text and develop it in the sermon, it opens the way. We arrive at it by asking theological questions to which we now turn.

We will close this chapter with a definition: The God sense of a biblical text may be defined as those dimensions of it that speak of God's nature, acts, and relationship to humanity and creation, and that enable the Bible to be read as Scripture, the book of the church. The God sense is not a singular meaning but many meanings. Narrowly, it refers to the particular God-focused sentence that the preacher identifies as the theme sentence of the sermon. Broadly it refers to the development of that understanding in the sermon and to any authentic theological meaning(s) of a text arrived at through a process of historical, literary, and theological exegesis. We now turn to the process of theological exegesis.

CHAPTER FIVE

Theological Exegesis
and the Literal Sense

This chapter demonstrates four practices that arise from having a double-literal sense. It shows how to: perform theological exegesis, allow the nature of the Word to affect sermon development, present God in a lively way in the sermon, and present the biblical text effectively in the sermon.

Some scholars get upset with a term like "theological exegesis" and insist that exegesis is reserved for historical-critical endeavor. We maintain that theological meanings genuinely reside in the text and only by their presence does the Bible function as Scripture. We need to determine what method best extracts them. Exegesis is a means of interrogating a text: When we ask historical questions of a biblical text, we evaluate it as a historical document from historical perspectives using relevant extracanonical materials for assistance. The same process applies to theological exegesis. We determine theological questions to ask the biblical text that include and go beyond those we ask to determine our theme sentence (that is, what God has done, is doing, and has promised to do), which will yield data to support it in the sermon.

Theological Exegesis

Following are thirty basic theological questions that preachers can use to help them begin to discern the revealed word in Scripture. They are central to theological criticism. Some of them overlap, and not every text is able to answer each question:

1. What is God (in one of the persons of the Trinity) doing in this biblical text?
2. What is God doing behind this biblical text, in the larger story?

3. What group or person represents God in this text?
4. What does this text say about God's identity?
5. What does this text say about human identity?
6. What does this text say about how humanity has fallen short of God's purposes?
7. What sin does this text reveal?
8. What divine judgment upon that sin does this text reveal?
9. What human brokenness or vulnerability does this text reveal?
10. What divine judgment rests upon those in this text who inflict brokenness or who take advantage of the vulnerable?
11. What change must the people make in the text?
12. Why does God choose to act?
13. What hope does this text imply or offer?
14. What action of God communicates that hope?
15. What does this text say about God's will for human beings?
16. What does this text say about how God will restore humanity to God's purpose?
17. What does this text say about God's love?
18. What does God do in this text to provide or accomplish what is needed?
19. What does God do behind this text in the larger story to accomplish what is needed?
20. What is God enabling the people in the text to accomplish?
21. What does this text say or imply about God's future promises?
22. What verb best captures God's help (that is, what God does) in this passage?
23. What sentence with God as the subject best establishes the God sense?
24. What action of the people in this text makes it necessary for God to act in this way?
25. What other central biblical texts display similar actions of God?

26. What teaching/doctrine of the church most closely corresponds to the God sense here?
27. What aspect of that doctrine applies?
28. What does this text say, imply, anticipate, or echo about Jesus Christ?
29. How does this text connect theologically to the cross, resurrection, and ascension?
30. What does the fact of the resurrection say to this text?

Preachers ask these questions once historical-critical exegesis is underway, but need not wait until it is completed. As human beings, we are quite capable of keeping the two processes distinct if we do them on parallel tracks. There is some advantage in allowing, for instance, some of the historical and literary questions of historical criticism to interplay with theological questions. For example, *Who is in power in this text?* will identify an individual who has special responsibilities before God. *Who is oppressed in this text?* will identify an individual who likely comes under God's favor. Theological questions may be asked at different levels of textual interpretation—for example, at the level of the events as history or as they have been interpreted by an editor. For example, if one determines that the Gospel writer put particular words into Jesus' mouth, perhaps to interpret one of his parables, then theological reasons for that decision need to be determined: What is it about the person of Jesus Christ that leads the editor to make that change? What is the editor saying about God and the faith?

Trouble, Grace, and God

Theological criticism is concerned with ensuring that an overly narrow perspective on God is not brought to or found in the text. Augustine, in his *On the Spirit and the Letter* (c. 6) identifies law and grace as a separate "sense" of scripture. Since Paul with reinforcement from Luther, the God sense of Scripture has often been understood as bifocal, containing both law and gospel, judgment and hope, or trouble and grace.[1] Trouble puts the burden on humanity to act, to conform to God's will, to respond to God's command, to acknowledge brokenness and sin in human dealings with one another and creation, and to turn in repentance and dependence to

71

God for help. Grace is God's action in response to that trouble, expressed most fully in the life, death, resurrection, and ascension of Jesus Christ and experienced in God's present and promised action in and through the Holy Spirit.

One scholar voices an important common frustration with this notion of a bifocal word: "we lay the same stencil over every text, asking, Where is the law and gospel? rather than, What is God saying to his people? This rigid approach assures the congregation of an explication of judgment and grace whether this particular text offers it or not."[2] The point is valid and two responses can be made. First, we engage theological criticism of the Bible that reads individual texts by the light of the gospel message and reads the canon by the light of all the individual texts. The God of history is a God of both trouble and grace. When God's word is read without discerning what is gracious in judgment or what is troublesome that requires grace, one is reading God too narrowly. Second, trouble and grace are two sides of the same coin. Where one is present so is the other. As Barth said, the Word that condemns can be the same Word that saves. Whenever we split one from the other, we are in danger of misrepresenting the Word.

Too many preachers and teachers of preaching confuse trouble and grace with a sermonic form that moves from problem to solution. Apart from the erroneous equation of gospel with a simplistic solution to a problem, rather than a relationship with the risen Christ, distinction needs to be made between a form of sermon and a basic grammar of Christian faith. Trouble and grace can be a sermon form, yet this connection encourages preachers to assess this simply as one form among many. In fact, we are far more accurate to conceive of trouble and grace as the underlying grammar of any act of Christian theology and proclamation, whatever form we choose, whatever text we preach. This two-sided coin is not some arbitrary coin we mint; its two sides are the two inseparable expressions of God's love in the cross and resurrection. Once God's action is located in the biblical text, both trouble and grace are available to the discerning interpreter since they are two ways of considering the same Word. The interpreter has a choice to present the theme sentence in terms of either trouble or grace. If the interpreter finds only one or the other in a text, this is not simply the text speaking but, in large measure, the interpreter's limited training in dealing with these matters. While either burden or hope can be an expression of the literal sense of the text, both are needed to develop its fullest expression.

Homiletical reasons dictate that preachers choose for the theme sentence a dimension of God's action that expresses grace, otherwise the sermon may never get to grace. Trouble can be discussed *ad nauseam* without ever leading to God, as we see all too often in pulpits around the world that deliver moralistic, anthropocentric sermons that essentially leave God out. These sermons tell people what they have to do on their own resources, without offering what God offers on the cross. The powers and principalities of this world condemn without hope, but God in Christ through the Holy Spirit offers unconditional love and never destroys without building up, never corrects without giving the means for accomplishing what is required. Grace in the sermon demands trouble or sin as its precondition in order to avoid construal as irrelevant or "cheap grace," which, Bonhoeffer reminds us, costs God nothing. Thus, from a homiletical perspective, when the theme sentence of a biblical text focuses on God's grace, the preacher is more likely to include discussion of the trouble that is the occasion for God to act in that manner. The interpreter thus has a choice not only to focus on the God sense, but also to discern what dimension of God's action to emphasize. Even Psalm 120 ("In my distress I cry unto the Lord, that he may answer me: 'Deliver me, O Lord, from lying lips.'") does not turn the corner into grace yet still communicates grace: God is the Deliverer upon whom one may call. My theological tradition encourages me to seek God at work in situations of life, and I bring that expectation to situations in the biblical texts as well. Trouble and grace are every bit a part of the text.

Even as a biblical text normally yields trouble and grace, the sermon normally expresses both. Biblical interpretation leads a preacher to develop an image of the biblical text in the sermon. People have a right to expect correction and instruction at church, to have burdens laid upon them, to have the law applied. However, unless they realize that they need grace, grace may not mean much. They also have a right to have faith renewed through an encounter with the risen Christ and to experience again the lightness of Christ's yoke. As long as preaching ends in moralizing or in telling people what they must do out of their own resources, as long as preachers fail to cast congregations on the sufficiency of God's grace to fulfill their individual ministries, the sermon falls short. This is the shortfall of much biblical criticism and may serve as further encouragement for preachers to engage in theological criticism.

Is There a Real God in This Sermon?

In composing a sermon ask, "Is there a real God in this sermon?" Addressing this question is a further task of theological criticism. A real God is the One God of the Trinity who functions in the sermon not as a metaphor or simile for some generic abstract term like truth or love, nor as a rhetorical device used to manipulate listeners, an idea the congregation must apprehend, or a linguistic God who exists only within "the prison house of our language." Rather, the sermon offers a God who literally exists; whom the church recognizes as the One who created everything; who in Christ Jesus suffered and died on a cross and rose again for the purpose of our salvation; who is alive and rules over all; who is active in the power of the Holy Spirit; who gathers and nurtures the church; and who is present in it, strengthening and equipping God's children for lives of faith, service; and love. This personal God dares to come to people in and through the Word and sacraments. God may be found in the created order and never leaves people without signs of abiding grace.

Many preachers wish they had more passion. Passion in preaching is not so much an emotional issue as it is a theological one. It arises out of a preacher's strong awareness of the power of God and that God wants to accomplish something through the sermon. Congregations likewise can become passionate about God and their faith if preaching is an event in which they experience God judging and reconciling the world. Thus, preachers do not offer just an essay about God, ideas with which to engage, information concerning God, or doctrines to believe—all of which are good and have their place—they offer, in the first instance, a relationship with God. God is offering that.

Earlier we spoke of the need for preachers as historical critics to exercise historical imagination to conceive the historical situation of the text and its people. In the same manner, preachers as theological critics need theological imagination to speak about God's actions in and behind the biblical text. On a practical level, the specific understanding comes from the God sense of the biblical text and is signaled by the theme sentence. The preacher reconstructs an image of the text so that God's judgment and grace toward humanity are the focus. In other words, the higher literal sense, the preaching sense, is developed in dialogue with the church's larger understanding of the nature and person of God. The goal is to communicate a lively sense of God such as is found in the Bible.

In addition to portraying the actions of God in and behind the text, one of the best means of communicating this vital God is to portray God speaking in our sermons. If we always portray God as silent, how will seekers get a sense that God communicates? Caution is needed, for the relationship between the preacher's words and God's Word is not always identity, and how the Holy Spirit uses our words is not up to us. Still, we preach from the perspective of faith and knowledge, thus we are required to be bold, to take risks on behalf of God.

Preachers can use various devices to awaken listeners to the truth that God speaks:

1. If God is one of the direct speakers in the biblical text, this speech is particularly important to utter. Quote the words of the text. Whether or not God is an actual speaker, one can always quote what God has said from anywhere in the Bible, particularly words that come from the same book and obviously relate to what is going on in one's text. For example, in a sermon on Peter's commissioning at the end of the Gospel of John, one might say, as a sermon conclusion (leaving out the verse locations): Follow me, Jesus says, for without me you can do nothing (John 15:5). Follow me, I am the bread of life; whoever comes to me will never be hungry (John 6:35). Follow me, let not your hearts be troubled, neither let them be afraid (John 14:27). Follow me, for you can do all things in Christ through him who strengthens you (Phil. 4:13).

2. Preachers can speak for God—putting word's into God's mouth, as it were—when we understand God to be speaking through a text, person, or textual situation. So, instead of saying God is against injustice, we can say more forcefully, God says, "Enough. There has been enough injustice, and now it is time for my way." The biblical prophets often communicated what they had

heard God say using the words, "Thus says the Lord." In other words, a preacher can often make God, in one of the persons of the Trinity, a more evident player in the biblical text than God might seem to be at first historical glance.

3. Preachers can speak to God in the sermon in the form of a brief conversation. "Well, God, you have told us that you care for the needy. We are at a place where we need some sign of it." Such conversation can be modeled on the intimacy of prayer or of the Psalms.

4. Preachers can also speak as individuals who have heard God. For example, "Anyone who has ever called out for God in times of deep distress knows. . . ." This relates to the ethos or authenticity of the preacher or what we could also call the piety of the preacher. For preaching to be compelling, the preacher needs to communicate a lively relationship with God while avoiding self-righteousness of the Pharisee toward the publican.

An Example of Theological Imagination

Preachers can employ theology in a sermon and not use sufficient theological imagination to make the material come alive. There is little point in employing theology if it is not going to be communicated effectively. Following is an example of what I mean by theological imagination of the sort that is needed for preaching, taken from a sermon on Genesis 3:

> On the way out of Eden, Eve must have had a conversation with God, "O God, I know we have brought this upon ourselves. But is there no way we could stay, not for ourselves, but for the sake of our children?" We don't know exactly what she said, but we know something of how God answered. God said, "Eve, it breaks my heart that you have to leave. This is what I planned for you and Adam and your descendants. But Eve, when your teeth bit the fruit, your feet stood still, but you had already left, because when you bit the fruit, you lost your innocence. Now you know good and evil. When you lose your innocence, Eden does not exist anymore." Eve pondered God's words in her heart. "Well, God," Eve said, "I can stand leaving, if I must. I can

stand facing hardship, if I must. I can stand almost any-thing, if I can only know that I am not leaving you." In spite of messing up her own life, Eve knew what she needed, and she needed God. She needed God to walk with her and Adam out into the world, not to forsake them as they had forsaken God. She needed still to be able to call on God. She needed to have God answer in the middle of the night when she was anxious about her children. She needed God to be in charge of the world—to know that God would still heed her cries.

And, of course, her need is exactly what God has in mind. One of the most remarkable pictures of God found any-where in the Bible we discover immediately after God tells Adam and Eve what awaits them beyond Eden. It is a pic-ture of extraordinary love and devotion: The verse reads, "And the Lord God made garments of skins for the man and for his wife, and clothed them." What a loving picture that is: God sewing garments for beloved children as they leave home and head out for the school of hard knocks. "Eve, there is no turning back to a simpler life," God said in words God could also address to you and me when we have messed up. "You are leaving Eden, but you are not leaving my love. *Where can you go from my spirit? Or where can you flee from my presence? If you take the wings of the morn-ing and settle at the farthest limits of the sea, even there my hand shall lead you.* I am not finished with you. You may have messed up, but I still have purposes for you. My forgive-ness is from everlasting to everlasting. There is no wrong that you have done that I cannot work for good, for those who love me. I come that you might have life and have it abundantly."

The Literal Text and the Literary Text

Is there a biblical text in this sermon? This important question at first glance may seem trivial or obvious, for if a sermon is based on a biblical text, surely that text is present in the sermon. However, if just the theme sentence is present in the sermon, the text is not present. And, if a sermon quotes a biblical text and then goes in a different direction, that text is not effectively in the sermon, guiding its words. If a sermon makes no attempt to connect the text to our world, the text is present but not in an effective manner. How a text is presented in a sermon is a matter of vital concern to its interpretation; after all, the sermon is the interpretation. How is the God sense secured for preaching? We cannot engage careful exegesis and then leave the manner of the text's interpretation in the sermon entirely up to chance. In preaching there is no interpretation until we have effectively presented it.

The theme sentence or major concern of the text is important because, first, it is one pathway to the heart of the text, and second, the preacher develops it so as to make it central in the sermon. To do this, the preacher must reconstruct the text in the sermon such that it yields the desired understanding. It is easy to have unrealistic expectations of preachers (how much exegetical work they can do in a busy parish), of congregations (what their interest is), and of sermons (how much time can be devoted to biblical matters). There is no one, single way the biblical text should be used in a sermon. Rather, there is a range of possibilities with varying advantages or disadvantages that include:

1. Use the text by bringing its theme to use in the sermon. In this approach, the sermon is primarily devoted to applying the text to contemporary life. The preacher carries into the sermon the theme sentence, for example, "Paul would endure anything rather than have a weakness impede his preaching" (see 1 Cor. 9:12-27). This is placed at the beginning of the sermon in a deductive format, or at the end in an inductive format. This approach assumes that when a congregation hears a text read prior to the sermon they appropriate it; that is, it is established as a unity in their minds, and they are now ready to deal with it in its parts. This is rarely the case, and this approach may work best with texts about which little can be said by way of history and context, for instance a proverb like, "A fool despises a parent's instruction, but the one who heeds admonition is prudent" (Prov. 15:5).

2. Use the words and events of the text plus its analysis and commentary in the sermon. In this approach, analysis of the text follows setting the scene so that with Luke 18:35 the listeners are walking with Jesus outside Jericho and hear the blind man calling. A verse by verse expository form of preaching can be used or a nar-

rative that develops sections of a story or an argument. Ideally, each item discussed will still serve the one theme sentence derived from exegesis. Caution must be used, for as the number of points of focus increase, the sermon can become difficult to follow as both the theme sentence and unity are lost.

3. Take parts from several texts and apply them. Biblical texts on the same theme can be woven together in one sermon, each with its own exposition and/or application. This can be done with texts on a thematic basis and can be effective if the texts are the sort that do not need a lot of explanation—normally, a congregation can deal in a substantial way with only one text. (A thematic approach can be an alternative that uses many texts but visits none for long.) Primary dangers here are disunity and using texts as proof texts, bending texts to make them say what we want them to say. This approach can demand much of listeners since with each shift of text, the subject of the sermon seems to shift.

What we have in a sermon is not the text itself but an image or representation of it. This image invariably has been shaped by a variety of forces. When the text arrives in the sermon, it has been cut, removed from its context, taken apart, rearranged, reassembled, represented, analyzed, and applied. Every time we handle a text we change it. Even if we take a biblical text and read it word for word within the sermon, the text is affected by the new context in which we place it, the manner of our reading it, and the purpose to which it applies. The sermon contains only the likeness—strong or weak, image or trace (Derrida/Sausseur)—of the biblical text. Strictly speaking, it exists only in the Bible.

The purpose of this distinction is not to split hairs, for most of us have a general idea of what is meant by a text in a sermon. Rather it is to emphasize that in the sermon itself, we are always dealing with an image of the text, and some images are more adequate than others to bear the theological freight we ask of them. For example, exegesis for Bible class will speak well to few people. Development of the narrative plot will create a different image. A similar understanding of the text could produce an entirely different sermon. All of this is to say that biblical interpretation does not stop at the threshold of the sermon; it carries all of the way through sermon composition, and preachers today receive little help where it matters greatly.

We have already identified a few ways in which biblical texts are used in preaching. In closing this chapter we may also make several recommendations for what is most effective in developing the image of the text in the sermon.

1. Develop the image of primarily one biblical text in the sermon. To go into depth with more than one text may meet the preacher's need and miss the congregation's.

2. Spend up to one half of the sermon developing the image of the text. Assume that the congregation needs the biblical text to be reconstructed as we speak of it in order for them to get it firmly in their consciousness. Conceive of this as a movie and not as an essay about history. Quote the words of the text wherever this is helpful.

3. Use history to create the Bible events in a lifelike way. The sermon need not present the exegetical kitchen work done in preparing for the guests.

4. Use narrative as much as possible to develop what is said about the text and events behind it. Allow teaching, doctrine, and commentary to come through the narrative as opposed to having long, dense paragraphs of abstract prose. Use difficult abstract thought sparingly so that when it is used, the congregation is not moved to become exhausted.

5. Present an image of the text that is rooted in experience. Even doctrine should sound like lived experience in a sermon—the reflection on heartfelt issues, not the presentation of Newtonian physics. One of the remarkable strengths of much African American preaching is its ability to speak about biblical people, for instance Miriam and Moses, as though they are immediate relatives of the people who are present.

6. Use the theme sentence repeatedly as a means to anchor the image of the text in the sermon.

Recovering the Literary Text for the Sermon

The Reformation and Enlightenment helped the church recover the literary units of the Bible. Texts were read within their larger contexts. This process was given added impetus in the Romantic movement by the likes of Friedrich Schleiermacher and Samuel Taylor Coleridge, affecting individual preachers like Horace Bushnell, Phillips Brooks, and Frederick W. Robertson but not having major impact until the rise of narrative preaching in the late 1960s to 1980s. Departments of language and literature in the university, by then, experienced a second wave of Romantic influence fueled by literary critics like I. A. Richards, who promoted Coleridge's theories of metaphor, imagination, and artistic unity, which are essential to much contemporary art. Historical criticism rediscovers biblical texts as complete literary units but, ironically, is better at taking them apart than in treating them as coherent units. Literary criticism helps biblical scholars be better engaged by texts, and because it functions to make the text accessible in the current moment, it also provides a way to transcend the distance between past and present with which historical criticism is concerned.

The recovery of the literary text for the sermon is served by the recovery of the biblical story. Most texts are, at least in the words of Hans Frei, history-like, that is, their stories cannot be discarded, for they bear the meaning.[3] The word "story" need not be understood in its narrow sense as referring only to those texts that are story, for we are seeking the thickness of story—the lifelike situation in, around, or behind any text whether wisdom, saying, epistle, or psalm. The sermon introduces the listeners not to historical people themselves, for we do not have direct access to them, but, at best, to responsible and imaginative presentations of the biblical texts' characters, writers, editors, or original hearers.

Often, we cannot determine the actual historical setting of a text. Not all texts are equally history. The creation accounts in Genesis, when compared to the book of Revelation, have a different feel as history and a different kind of historicity. One can preach on Isaiah as one prophet, as three prophets—I, II, and III Isaiah, now contested—or as a canonical process (which probably multiplies "Isaiah" although it is hard to imagine how to present this effectively without resorting to speaking of Isaiah as one prophet). The congregation comes to church not to seek resolution of obscure historical issues but to know that they belong to God. Still, the events narrated in the Bible are rooted in the lives of real people who witness to a historical God.

History informs preaching in the same manner that it informs good movies. Movies present events in a lively and engaging way, though preachers need to avoid the distortions of history for which Hollywood is renowned. Rich sensory words used with economy can help make up for the lack of an actual camera. The first task with any new scene location is to give the location through visual details. Once this is established, focus on people in relationship wherever possible. Avoid being a slave to chronology: Do not start at the beginning of every story and work through to the end. Rather, focus on the place and time of the most significant action. Once that scene is well under way, important information from earlier events can be introduced by way of retrospection. Allow biblical truths and propositions to emerge through the action. We cannot be sure about weather, clothing, sequence, and the like, and though we strive to represent both history and the text faithfully, we seek a history capable of bearing the theological truth.

Events in the text ought not to become a subject of debate: Do not get Noah out in the ark only to question whether such an ark is possible, for the sermon will sink along with the ark. Preach the ark so that it floats. Even if rational explanations of the parting of the Red Sea or manna in the desert could be satisfying, they do not get closer to a theological understanding of the text—in fact, they serve only to remove God from the picture. Some preachers so dilute the miracles of Jesus that they end up comparing the blind man given sight to a person in a checkout line being given a smile and told to have a nice day: Even if the preacher claims that God motivates the smile, the comparison trivializes the text. Similarly, in some sermons the resurrection becomes a mere metaphor for something else instead of the event at the center of a Christian view of life. Instead of questioning whether miracles happen, preachers can strive to preach them so that they do happen in and through the sermon. In this manner the congregation is engaged at an existential level where they must decide whether they will profess the Lord as the One who encounters them in Scripture.

In this section we have been examining the literal sense of Scripture. In our next section we turn to consider the ancient methods of spiritual interpretation that, together with the theological literal sense, provide the model for theological interpretation today. We turn to the spiritual senses not to revive them, for they never died though they are denied, but to learn how we might use them to strengthen reading the Bible in theological ways. Although we move beyond the higher literal sense, we continue to explore the God sense of Scripture.

PART II
Spiritual Readings:
Homiletical Criticism

The allegory shows us where our faith is hid;
The moral meaning gives us rules of daily life;
The anagogy shows us where we end our strife.
—Augustine of Dacia

CHAPTER SIX

The Spiritual Senses:
An Introduction

The ancient spiritual senses are yet further ways to talk about the theological component or God sense of the biblical text. In their contemporary form they are authentic theological meanings that make specific connections with congregational needs and practical life. Our forebears have much to teach us about theological interpretation; we have not paid sufficient attention to what they said because we assume that what they called spiritual interpretation is dead and gone. In fact, when the literal sense becomes the only sense, spiritual interpretation simply goes underground. It allows preachers to make important links with faith and life: the moral sense anticipates the gospel call for a change in life; the allegorical sense speaks to the essential role of doctrine in preaching; and the prophetic sense addresses the need for the end times to inform life in the present. Together they remind us that when we approach Scripture for purposes of preaching, our work is not complete if we have not addressed these issues. We do not have to duplicate their methods in order to achieve their goals.

We do not now move to a different realm of interpretation as the word "spiritual" implies and Origen intends when he connects the literal sense with the physical body and the other senses with the Spirit. This use of "spiritual" originated when theology was not yet developed. Spiritual now often connotes something revealed, intuited, or private that does not easily submit to reason, yet spiritual exegesis was based in reason. As Hugh of St. Victor notes, the literal sense can contain that which contradicts or "which smacks of the absurd or the impossible. But the spiritual meaning admits no opposition; in it, many things can be different from one another, but none can be opposed."[1] The spiritual senses represent the best rational rules our ancestors could devise for faithful and coherent rendering of Scripture. Studying them today can add to the vibrancy and depth of our sermons.

The three spiritual senses provide lenses for viewing a text. They often overlap. To overhear Gregory the Great, the manner of their use on a specific theme is flexible and spontaneous:

> [The expositor who] treats of sacred writ should follow the way of a river, for if a river, as it flows along its channel, meets with open valleys on its side, into these it immediately turns the course of its current, and when they are copiously supplied, presently it pours itself back into its bed. Thus unquestionably, thus should it be with everyone that treats of the Divine Word, that if, in discussing any subject, he chance to find at hand any occasion of seasonable edification, he should, as it were, force the streams of discourse towards the adjacent valley, and when he has poured forth enough upon its level of instruction, fall back into the channel of discourse which he had proposed to himself.[2]

The spiritual senses survive today and have evolved into the third unit of the trinity of biblical criticisms that constitute homiletics: homiletical criticism. Like historical and theological criticism, homiletical criticism is a practice of scholarly biblical interpretation. It develops the gospel message from a biblical text, locates it within the contemporary world, and communicates its meaning effectively (with attention to rhetoric and poetics) to the congregation. The spiritual senses are a concrete reminder that biblical texts have many legitimate theological meanings that keep being uncovered both from age to age and throughout the sermon process. They are shaped even as the sermon is composed and delivered. All of our theological senses (including the higher literal sense) dwell in the text itself, though we cannot make this claim of all the spiritual interpretations of our ancestors.

Biblical interpretation is already some distance from the condition David Steinmetz identified in 1980 when he despaired of the single meaning sought by historical criticism and pointed to the superiority of the medieval multiple senses as an alternative:

> How was a French parish priest in 1150 to understand Psalm 137, which bemoans captivity in Babylon, makes rude remarks about Edomites, expresses ineradicable longing for a glimpse of Jerusalem, and pronounces a blessing on anyone who avenges the destruction of the temple by dashing Babylonian children against a rock? The priest lives in Concale, not Babylon, has no

personal quarrel with Edomites, cherishes no ambitions to visit Jerusalem (though he might fancy a holiday in Paris), and is expressly forbidden by Jesus to avenge himself on his enemies. Unless Psalm 137 has more than one possible meaning, it cannot be used as a prayer by the church and must be rejected as a lament belonging exclusively to the piety of ancient Israel.[3]

Steinmetz was thinking only in terms of historical criticism that operates through time (diachronic) and offers only one meaning. Today (indeed even in 1980), literary and rhetorical analysis of such texts offers many meanings within historical criticism as well as more direct access to the texts as texts in the present (synchronic) moment. Twenty years have provided remarkable movement.

Nonetheless, we are likely to view the spiritual senses narrowly, as "applications" of the text to the purposes of the church, rather than as genuine meanings to which the text leads through means that commonly are more synchronic than diachronic. When a biblical text is "applied" to our situation, in this way of thinking, a comparison or analogy is made. For example we say, "The biblical people are stubborn, and so are we." History must ensure that the basis of our analogy is valid, that we are not presuming a similarity when in fact the historical situation is vastly different. Historical criticism appropriately expands the biblical text and uses whatever historical materials are deemed relevant to establish the text's meaning. These materials become branches grafted onto the limbs of the text, so to read it as though the branches are not there, leads to error.

Historical criticism brings history to the text just as theological criticism brings tradition and doctrine, especially concerning the Bible as the Word of God. Homiletical criticism, using contemporary versions of the spiritual senses, similarly expands the text and asks questions shaped by the faith and life of the ongoing community of faith, often using contextual theologies. Of course, these three criticisms overlap in places. Each type requires its own kind of imagination: Historical imagination requires a lively sense of the biblical period; theological imagination requires a lively sense of God; and homiletical imagination requires a keen sense of contemporary people living in diverse circumstances, thus it includes moral and social justice issues, issues concerning salvation and the Realm of God, and issues of appropriate doctrine. Each type of criticism has its dangers: Historical criticism on its own makes the text a-theological and turns Scripture into history; theological criticism on its own makes the text a-historical and turns Scripture into dogma; and homiletical criticism on its own turns Scripture into ideology, therapy, or cultic practice. These three types of critical endeavor are largely parallel tracks.

Each type of practice has its own integrity that follows textual prompts to accomplish its objective. It is wrong to think that historical criticism belongs to Bible class and theological criticism to theology class because each of these classes often defines its tasks and objectives as different from what best serves the needs of preaching. With fragmentation of the theological curriculum, preaching can no longer be assumed to have priority in seminaries. Moreover, each of these classes necessarily combines history, theology, and the present in its own way and has its own purposes in doing so. In homiletics our three types of criticism are not separate consecutive steps: There is certainly some progression from historical, but they are largely simultaneous. The poorest preachers are those who confuse any one of these types of criticism as the whole task, just as the best of preachers attend to integrating all three.

A clarification is needed: Medieval literature frequently discusses the moral and allegorical senses, but little is written about the third spiritual sense—the prophetic sense—also known as the anagogical (meaning "to lead up"), or mystical sense, that has to do with eschatology, soteriology, and the ascent of the soul to union with Christ. The paraphrase of Augustine of Dacia's verse reads: The anagogy shows us where we end our strife. Many ancient rhymes and discussions mention anagogy; it is included in the normal listing of the four senses, yet few writers, ancient or contemporary, say much about it. Most of the preachers use it, however, and use it frequently, often as a way to warn about the consequences of backsliding and unfaithful living.

The reason for this relative silence is hard to establish, for the prophetic sense is essential to their way of reading the Bible. We may understand prophetic sense in two ways: (1) any sense that allows an Old Testament text to be understood as being about Christ who is the fulfillment of the law (Matt. 5:17) and (2) anagogy that, in either Testament, points to last things we await at the end of time. A clear distinction exists between the two, which makes it hard to understand why our ancestors often dropped reference to the second. One reason may be this: When anagogy is employed to find a meaning about the end times in texts not literally dealing with that subject, allegory is the method that must be employed, thus the allegorical sense overtakes the anagogical.

There is a related reason. Many biblical texts literally speak directly of the final things: How life is to end, Christian hope, the realm of God, salvation and damnation, the wolf lying down with the lamb—matters that we commonly consider under the doctrine of eschatology—and many other texts have related themes. Throughout history, entire worship services have gathered around these themes at funerals, services in penitential seasons of the church year such as Advent and Lent, and services of evangelism that often use some of the more frightening eschatological texts to entice people into faith.[4] Since "prophecy" plays such a large part in the Bible and church life, to include a "prophetic sense" in how to read the Bible is both obvious and necessary. Still, over the centuries it has not been so obvious that everyone referred to anagogy or singled it out for special attention. Origen has only three senses—body, soul, and spirit. Thomas Aquinas argues that while Augustine speaks of four senses, his first three (history; etiology [cause of behavior or action]; analogy to other Scripture) are literal: "Of the four . . . allegory stands alone for the three spiritual senses of our exposition."[5] Hugh of St. Victor has only three (history, allegory, and tropology [moral]).[6] De Lubac shows that by the medieval age, only these three senses of Scripture were commonly named.[7]

Allegory, we know, has to do with doctrine, in particular with Christ and what is believed. Giles of Paris writes poetically of only three senses and says of allegory, "whoever drinks this wine of Scripture hunts for Jesus and finds him, reaching him on the wooded heights."[8] What is the difference in interpretative strategy between reaching Jesus "on the wooded heights" (allegory) and reaching Jesus at the end of time (prophecy)? As we will see, the prophetic sense is so closely related to allegory that it may have been difficult to separate in theory or practice. For that matter, could the moral sense be separated from the prophetic since discussion of moral living was often in terms of its consequences in damnation or salvation? Understood in this way, allegory is a technique, and the prophetic and moral senses are functions of it.

If these are not precise questions our ancestors asked, the questions at least point to our difficulty in speaking of a separate, prophetic sense with more confidence than they demonstrated. Four senses persist in medieval literature, in part because of tradition—so deep is fourfold exegesis in the culture and mind-set—and in part because of the prophetic sense being practiced frequently whenever death and the end times are the lenses used to read Scripture. For these various reasons, anagogy, here, is given less attention than the other spiritual senses and is discussed under allegory and from a practical homiletical perspective for today.

Concerning the order we give to the senses, some medieval sources argue for a move from literal to allegorical to moral, and still others place moral before allegorical, as we will do here, not only to save the most difficult for last but also to recognize that allegory as it is traditionally understood provides no solid basis for either morals or doctrine.

CHAPTER SEVEN
The Moral Sense

The Enlightenment marked the end of fourfold exegesis, yet the spiritual senses have continued, though unacknowledged and underground, with different names. The moral sense is no exception, and it continues to thrive today because sermons naturally have a moral purpose: They try to change lives and influence people to act in certain ways. It provides guidance on Christian life, as in Augustine of Dacia's verse, "The moral meaning gives us rules of daily life." It is also known as the tropological sense, trope meaning "turn" or "turning," in this case turning a text to moral purpose.

In medieval thought, this sense addressed not only morality but also the purpose of life, which was spiritual growth in conformity with Jesus Christ. Thus, it was also known as the "soul" sense. In John Cassian's exegesis of "Jerusalem," Jerusalem literally is the city; allegorically is the church; morally is the human soul; and prophetically is the heavenly city of God. A further verse from the Middle Ages on the word "manna" helps to stress the spiritual side: "Manna may be taken *literally*, for the food miraculously given to the Israelites in the wilderness; *allegorically*, for the Blessed Sacrament in the Eucharist; *tropologically*, for the spiritual sustenance of the soul day by day through the power of the indwelling Spirit of God; and *anagogically*, for the food of blessed souls in heaven—the Beatific Vision and perfected union with Christ."[1] The connection between the moral sense and the soul is, of course, that immoral behavior jeopardizes the soul even as nurture of the soul is necessary for living a moral life.

Our early church ancestors including Paul struggled with how to connect with the Old Testament in light of Christ. We see this in Paul's Letter to the Romans as he wrestles with the validity of the law. They found Christ in the Old Testament, proved Christ from it, and understood that all Jewish institutions pointed to Christ; thus they accomplished two purposes: They utilized the Old

Testament as a basis for their doctrine, and they accepted Jewish laws of morality.

We might naïvely think they found a moral reading of Scripture only in the moral teachings of Scripture interpreted as law; for example, the Decalogue, the Sermon on the Mount, Romans 12, Colossians 3:18-25, and 1 Peter 2:1-17 are passages that deal with moral instruction or exhortation to right living (i.e., paraenesis). In our age, interpretation for moral purpose does not always seem wise or possible with every biblical text. This was not the understanding of our ancestors because, for them, the primary purpose of Scripture was moral edification through knowledge of the love of God. To read Scripture in a way that did not correspond with this was evil. Again, at the heart of medieval exegesis is 2 Corinthians 3:6, "for the letter kills, but the Spirit gives life." Augustine, in *On Christian Doctrine* (III), cautions readers not to take figurative expressions literally. On the other hand, if a text is unedifying in its literal sense, it is to be understood figuratively. The purpose of biblical exegesis is found in 1 Corinthians 13:13, to teach faith (what is to be believed or allegory), hope (what is to be lived for or prophecy), and charity or love (what is to be done or the moral sense), of which the greatest is love.[2] Augustine advises preachers to study the text "until an interpretation contributing to the reign of charity is produced,"[3] thus for him, a passage is not rightly understood until it has a moral interpretation that contributes to the rule of love.

When the literal addresses faith, hope, and love it functions the same way as the spiritual senses that are real extensions of the higher literal. These moral themes are to be taken literally (II, 9) and even when a text does not address them, they are to be sought by untying the "knot...of...figurative action" (II, 14). The literal also is what kills in contrast to "the life-giving law of the Spirit" (Rom. 8:2 NEB). Since the aim of law must be love, interpreters seek the meaning of the Old Testament in the New, in the love of Christ dying on the cross and being raised again.

The moral sense is distinct from all the other senses in that it leads to virtuous behavior through meditation, contemplation, prayer, and good works. The other senses by contrast lead to knowledge. Did the ancient moral sense include personal and community responsibility, as ours does? For the most part, it was focused on the individual's rightness before God that contributes to unity with Christ, yet all of this was preached in the context of a far less individualistic society than our own. Many of the homilies of John Chrysostom (ca. 347–407) follow a two-part format, particularly his fifty-five Homilies on Acts. They move from exegesis in the first part to moral exhortation in the second. Often the second part seems unrelated to the text in the first part, for instance, seven homilies preach on swearing. Amanda Berry Wylie finds greater unity in this than many other scholars find: "In the first half of each homily... [John] emphasizes the actions and the personalities of the apostles as patterns or models for all Christians. The second half of each homily then addresses specific moral virtues or the way that we ought to live. One part shows us by example, the other tells us directly."[4] The sermons lead to moral behavior essentially by providing the congregation with knowledge and guidelines they may follow.

For the ancients, nearly any text led to moral purpose, often by linking it to Christ. For example, Ambrose of Milan (ca. 340–397) uses a christological interpretation of a psalm to encourage virginity:

> Virgin, take wings, but wings of the Spirit, so that you may soar above the vices if you desire to reach Christ. "He dwells on high and looks upon the lowly" (Ps. 113:5). And his appearance is that of a cedar of Lebanon whose foliage is in the clouds while its roots are set in the earth. For its beginning is from heaven, its ending is on earth, and it produces its fruit nearest heaven. Search all the more diligently for so excellent a flower.[5]

Gregory I, the Great (540–604) writes extensively on moral behavior, not only in his *Pastoral Rule*, which is really instruction to the entire church, but also in his *Moral Reflections on the Book of Job*, where he identifies the "seven deadly sins" as pride, covetousness, lust, envy, gluttony, anger, and sloth. He is also concerned with care of the individual soul and cautions about the dangers of following the literal meanings because sometimes "they convey no sort of instruction to the reader, but only engender error" (*Moral Reflections*, 1:7). He compares various texts that have similar spiritual "testimonies" as a way to determine correct behavior. The book of Job (who is viewed as a type of Christ) became an important book for medieval moral instruction. Aquinas also wrote on it.

For him, the moral sense occurred "whenever things in the New Testament explicitly ascribed or referred to Christ are further signs of what we ourselves ought to do."[6] The historical sense of the text in its prophetic capacity points to unfolding events in each succeeding age, including the age of Christ in which their meaning as signs and characters becomes evident. Thus, the Old Testament becomes a means by which to read the New Testament instead of just the other way around.

Normally, in the medieval period, the moral sense was found through emphasis of biblical commands and in identifying and imitating Christ, as is clear in Thomas à Kempis's influential *Imitation of Christ*, a book of prayer, devotional aids, and meditations on spiritual growth. In this model, Christ is essentially an example, and it is up to humans to live like him. Biblical characters also function as examples of moral behavior to the degree that they anticipate or are examples of the ideal of Christ. The moral sense often includes allegory, and characters in the Bible are taken as codes that represent abstract qualities. Thomas of Chobham in the late–twelfth century indicates how this can work: "One thing is understood through another in a tropological way when it is made to convey moral instruction *(moralis instructio)* or when by *transumptio* 'night', for example, signifies sin and 'day' signifies virtue."[7]

Hugh of St. Victor sees a theological danger in the moral sense, and thus seeks a balance between works and grace: "It then remains for you to gird yourself for good work, so that what you have sought in prayer you may merit to receive in your practice. God wishes to work with you; you are not forced, but you are helped. If you are alone, you accomplish nothing; if God alone works, you have no merit."[8] As historical consciousness increases, the Old Testament characters begin to emerge from behind their stories in something resembling three-dimensional form. They begin to function not just as examples to follow or mere symbols and types of virtue or vice. They are seen, at least by Luther, as real-life people whose lives and faith then can be compared to life now. By this move to analogy from mere imitation to comparison of their struggles with ours, God's role in the process of a character's spiritual growth comes into focus. For Luther, the Old Testament comes to stand on its own as a positive model for Christian faith.

Analogy is used with people in the Old Testament in terms not only of their obedience to the law but also of their faith in God. As Luther says of the ten lepers commanded by Jesus to show themselves to the priest to fulfill Jewish law (Luke 17:14), "the account . . . does not pertain to me. The example of their faith, however, does pertain to me; I should believe Christ, as did they."[9] His reason is the cruci-fixion and resurrection in which Christ acts radically for us and accomplishes everything necessary for salvation. The moral sense changes with Luther, as one scholar observes, from an anthro-pocentric *what we do* to a Christocentric *what God does for us on our behalf.*[10] Even in his last lectures on Genesis, Luther remains largely moral in emphasis.

The Moral Sense and Preaching

Throughout history the moral sense was broadly associated with preaching in that it met the needs of even the simplest people. Even in ancient Jewish homiletics, the term *peshat* refers to the plain sense or the literal meaning and *derash* refers to the homiletical sense or the moral meaning.[11] The late–Middle Ages associated the literal sense with grammar and history; the allegorical sense with theology; and the moral sense with preaching. Preaching was pri-marily moral instruction in faith and good behavior, yet it also employed the other senses, as did theology. The preaching manu-als of the twelfth and thirteenth centuries assisted local preachers with the four senses as well as other devices for composing ser-mons including startling imagery, anecdotes, crude histories, alle-gory, moral stories, conjecture, and some treatment of biblical texts. Allegory or doctrinal reflection was too difficult for most local preachers, and they needed whatever assistance they could obtain. In the late–medieval period, preaching was regarded as the highest form of biblical study: Allan of Lille, who in 1200 wrote the first textbook on preaching since Augustine, places preaching as the seventh and highest rung of scriptural study.[12] In this age, *Lectio* was the reading of a lesson with use of commentary; *Disputatio* was Anselm's typical form of medieval lecture or disputation on prob-lematic texts that commonly moved from questions to arguments against a position to arguments for it; and *Predicatio,* or preaching, was moral instruction that not only gave the sense of the text but also explained what it and other related texts meant in terms of practical life.

Moral instruction takes several forms including character study. Augustine's comments on Psalm 3 provide an instance of negative moral example in the linking of Absalom and Judas as similar character types. Christ serves as a positive moral example in his patience and love toward Judas:

> And when the history of the New Testament shows us the great, the truly wonderful forbearance of our Lord, who bore with Judas so long just as though he were upright, and although He was aware of his designs yet admitted him to the feast in which He set before and entrusted to His disciples His own body and blood under a figure [i.e., a type], who finally in the other's very act of betrayal accepted his kiss [Matt. 26:49], we can easily see that Christ showed nothing but peace toward the man who betrayed Him, although the traitor's heart was prey to intentions so criminal. Absalom, then, is termed "peace of his father" because his father cherished the peace which the son lacked.[13]

Andrew of St. Victor (ca. 1150) writes in praise of the character of Isaiah:

> That he was noble and of royal blood, is clearly proved, if Jewish tradition is true, by the marriage between his daughter and Manasses, the son of Ezechias king of Juda. His dignity of office lies in the fact of his being a prophet.... Plain proof of his worth and holiness is that he merited to see the Lord, as he writes himself; that his lips were cleansed by a live coal, brought from the altar by a seraph's hand; and chiefly that God testifies to Isaias being his servant, of whom he says: *as my servant hath walked, naked and barefoot* [Isa. xx. 3].
>
> His firm, enduring constancy, his intention to declare the truth, his courage in foretelling disaster to princes and peoples, kings and priests, lands and nations, towns, villages, cities, and camps, these shine out clearly in the prophet's death, and the torments worse than death that he underwent.[14]

A shift took place in moral instruction in the latter part of the Middle Ages toward outward behavior and social criticism as preachers addressed social and religious abuse. Humor was used in the form of satire with a type of story known as *exempla* that typically ridiculed individuals or entire classes of people in a manner that most congregations would not tolerate today, not least because of the threat of lawsuits. There was no loyalty to fellow Christians in this; friars and monks typically accused each other of all manner of licentious behavior. Such preaching proved to be popular, entertaining, and apparently, an effective means of instruction.

Meister Eckhart, preaching on Luke 10:38, turns the plain meaning on its head and makes Martha to be the good moral example. He attributes much virtue to Martha and allows Mary virtue only after she later learns to serve following Jesus' ascension:

> Mary was a Martha before she became a Mary, for when she sat at the feet of our Lord, she was not Mary. . . . But Martha was very steadfast in her being and hence she said, "Lord, tell her to get up," as if to say, "Lord, I would wish that she were not sitting there just for the pleasure of it. I would like her to learn life so that she might possess it in being. Tell her to get up, so that she might become perfect." Her name was not really Mary as she sat at Christ's feet. This is what I call Mary: a well-disciplined body obedient to a wise soul. Obedience is when the will satisfactorily carries out what insight commands. . . .
>
> Now some people want to go so far as to achieve freedom from works. I say this cannot be done.... "Mary sat at the feet of the Lord and listened to his words," and learned, for she had just been put into school and was learning to live. But afterwards, when she had learned and Christ had ascended into heaven and she received the Holy Spirit, then she really for the first time began to serve.[15]

With Luther and Calvin, by contrast, the moral sense arises out of the literal text and focuses on life in faith before God. Calvin on Psalm 3 finds David to be a model of faith and trust in the full sufficiency of God's grace.[16] Calvin preaches on 2 Timothy 2:16-18 (esp., "Among them are Hymenaeus and Philetus who have swerved from the truth by claiming that the resurrection has already taken place"), and develops a negative model:

> When he nameth Hymeneus, and Philetus, he showeth that we must not spare them, who, like scabby sheep, may infect the flock, but we must rather tell every one, what kind of men they are, that

they may beware of them.... Those who endeavor to turn every thing upside down, will come and sow their false doctrine among the people, in order to draw them into a contempt of God. These barking dogs, these vile goats, these ravenous wolves, are they that have erred, and endeavored to overthrow the faith of the church: and yet we suffer them.... We see the flock of God troubled and tormented with ravenous wolves, that devour and destroy whatsoever they can. Must we be moved with mercy towards a wolf; and in the mean time let the poor sheep and lambs of which our Lord hath such a special care, let them, I say, perish?[17]

For Luther, the moral sense is of limited value, for while it sets before people the actions or lives they are to complete, it does not, in fact, assist them. He says concerning 1 Peter 4: " 'Christ suffered for us, thereby leaving us an example.' Thus when you see how he prays, fasts, helps people, and shows them love, so also you should do, both for yourself and for your neighbor. However this is the smallest part of the gospel, on the basis of which it cannot yet even be called gospel."[18] Luther equates moral instruction with law, and justification is "by faith apart from works" (Rom. 3:28). The chief value of setting moral instruction before people is to help them not only understand the law and to guide them in the direction of right behavior, but also to understand the significance of what Christ accomplished on the cross by dying for them, without whom no good can be done. The good works people do are only with God's help. Luther explains the relationship between faith and works:

> Thus we have it that faith justifies without any works; and yet it does not follow that men are, therefore, to do no good works, but rather that the true works will not be absent. Of these, the work-righteous saints know nothing, but feign works of their own in which there is no peace, joy, confidence, love, hope, boldness, nor any of the qualities of true Christian works and faith.
>
> He [Christ] teaches us that by faith we are not so freed from sin that we can be idle, slack, and careless, as though there were no longer any sin in us. There is sin; but it is no longer counted for condemnation, because of the faith that strives against it.[19]

With Luther a new category of moral sense is born that is intolerant of (a) altering the literal meaning of texts to moral purposes,

(b) destroying faith by turning the gospel into human laws, and (c) conceiving of good works as anything other than that which is enabled by faith and freedom on behalf of the neighbor.[20]

The Moral Sense as Method

How can preachers use the moral sense today? Legitimate moral significance lies within a biblical text as part of its fabric. Hayden White claims that every historian draws upon ideological considerations to explain what is described and to give it unity of argument and plot, and this unity he labels as moral or aesthetic: "the moral implications of a given historical argument have to be drawn from the relationship which the historian presumes to have existed *within* the set of events under consideration."[21] Different literary genres yield different ideological thrusts; thus in the tragic mode, one historian might imply the need for social accommodation while another the need for heroism and militancy. In other words, the moral dimension of a work resides within a text's narrative fabric and cannot be reduced simply to propositional or constructive affirmations.

Proper use of the moral sense does not include pursuing a moral that connotes a violence to the text. Drawing a legitimate moral from a text is one thing and moralizing is another. Moralizing turns the message of a biblical text into what people must do when the text does not say it or when the text does not give moral instruction, without regard for what God accomplishes in Jesus Christ.

Preachers generally move from a particular biblical text to a specific contemporary situation and often apply a moral understanding. Ethicists read the Bible in a similar manner when they conceive of Scripture theologically as "revealed morality." An ethicist commonly finds general tendencies in various biblical texts and, by them, establishes ethical principles. James M. Gustafson identifies four standard principles that ethicists use to guide how they discern morality with Scripture, and he notes problems inherent to each that apply to preaching. The options for employing the Bible to moral purpose are limited:

1. Uphold the Ideal of Love. Augustine develops this principle that involves searching a biblical text for the loving interpretation. What is the drawback? Both sides on a controversial issue such as war can appeal to it.

2. Uphold Moral Ideals. People are judged by their ability to uphold moral ideals given in Scripture. However, given the conflicting literal statements about morality within Scripture, Gustafson questions whether there is scriptural warrant for a "language of moral ideals."

3. Avoid Behavior That the Bible Condemns. People and groups are judged to be morally wrong if their behavior resembles behavior that the Bible in similar circumstances condemns. Unfortunately, this principle of moral analogy is not straightforward. If one moves from current events to seek biblical texts in determining what is right, one is likely to find texts that confirm one's viewpoint. If one moves from Scripture to current events, "then one is faced with the persistent question of which events are most nearly consistent with certain central tendencies of the biblical, theological, and moral witness. One would have to decide whether the Hebrew wars of conquest of Canaan were 'truer' to the central themes of biblical morality than was the liberation accomplished by the Exodus."[22] Gustafson notes that Calvinists in South Africa used the analogy of the chosen people's right to the land of the Canaanites when they expanded into the territory of the Africans in the nineteenth century.

4. Obey Specific Biblical Norms and Principles. People are judged by selected moral values, norms, and principles found in many different kinds of biblical literature. A problem here is again the lack of a normative standard when a variety of norms and standards exists in Scripture.[23]

In light of the problems with each strategy, he seeks a "theological and ethical principle [that] would have to be judged as normative for the whole of scriptural witness."[24] He finds it in "the idea of a 'God who acts.' "[25] This is, of course, the same God-statement that homiletics uses in identifying the literal sense of a biblical text. Daniel Patte, in his recent *Ethics of Biblical Interpretation: a Reevaluation*, argues that ethicists can no longer claim objectivity or universal status for their scriptural interpretations and must concede and acknowledge legitimate contrasting viewpoints. He advocates continued practice of historical-critical method, a readiness to identify contrasting interpretations, and an assumption of "responsibility for our choice of one reading as the most significant for us."[26] His advice is good for preachers who, in particular, must take responsibility for the positions they take, including the choice of a God-centered reading when many biblical critics argue against it. On ethical issues one cannot claim to have the final word. Moreover, preachers need to indicate alternative positions even as they put forward their own. If preaching on a controversial issue, for example, a preacher can honor people on both sides who have arrived at their perspective in good faith. In other words there is a difference between moral instruction that establishes law and ethical preaching that sets alternatives before people in balanced ways.

In both homiletics and ethics, the God sense, or God-statement, is only an instrument for direction. Ethicists develop approaches on generalized themes of who God is, what God says, and what God does, for instance: Christ is liberator (black, womanist, feminist, and liberationist theologians); or God is hope (Jürgen Moltmann); or Jesus as Pacifist (Dorothy Day); or Jesus as Lord (Lesslie Newbigin). Ethicists commonly move from these themes to an evaluative description of their contemporary situation. Preachers at times move in the same direction, in fact, they come to Scripture already shaped by theological and ethical viewpoints that influence how they image the text in the sermon even if this influence is not intentionally identified, cultivated, or specifically articulated. Normally, preachers also move in another direction, from a particular claim about God heard in the text and coherent with the revelation of the triune God in Scripture, to particularization, concretization, and actualization in the community. The overriding sermon theme becomes an ethical guide: Because God acts in particular ways, we are called to conform our actions to God's will. Conceiving of this requires moral imagination, the willingness to imagine being someone else in need and to contemplate the moral consequences of action.

The Moral Sense in Practice

Peter J. Gomes, writing for the *New York Times*, recently identified the best sermon of the last one thousand years: It was given by Governor Winthrop of the Massachusetts Bay Colony in 1630. (Gomes may demonstrate a touch of myopia in choosing a hometown sermon.) The sermon is titled "Christian Charity: A Model Hereof," and is based on Matthew 5:13-16 from the Sermon on the

Mount. Winthrop uses the "city set on a hill" as a metaphor of America, a nation exemplary in virtue and mutual support. Gomes says of it, "What runs through his sermon . . . is an honest realization that the seductions of self-interest and ambition are as dangerous to the common good as famine and pestilence."[27] This is typical of moral preaching in history; Winthrop preaches morality from a text on morality ("In the same way, let your light shine before others, so that they may see your good works and give glory to your Father in heaven"—Matt. 5:16). In such cases the literal meaning offers direction for living.

There can be both ethics in Scripture and an ethical use of Scripture. If preaching on ethics, we need to use texts that correspond as closely as possible to the ethical issue at hand. The moral sense is usually reserved for those parts of Scripture that do not exhort people to live moral lives. Our ancestors understood that ethical issues and moral instruction were not restricted to explicitly moral texts. Many texts lead to some form of ethical issue or moral invitation, as medieval Christians were keenly aware. The issue can be any action of love, perhaps taking meals to shut-ins or visiting someone in the hospital. Whether this issue is an invitation for faithful living or a command determines if the biblical text is being used for moral purpose or for moralizing.

Preaching morality without God leaves individuals utterly reliant upon their own resources which, if adequate, remove any need for Christ. Thus preachers who fail to develop the biblical text's "God sense" often end up with moralistic sermons. Proverbs 11:25 is a moral text: "A generous person will be enriched, and one who gives water will get water." Is it true? Can a generous person not become poor? At a literal level the text endorses generosity as a means to get rich. If the faithful preacher refuses this meaning, she or he goes beyond historical criticism into theological criticism and looks in the surrounding verses for clues to an alternative understanding. Verse 24 does not offer it: "Some give freely, yet grow all the richer"; however, verses 28 ("Those who trust in their riches will wither") and 30 ("The fruit of the righteous is a tree of life") imply that verse 25 speaks of riches beyond material wealth. Thus in terms of faith, a generous person becomes rich, obtaining the tree of life. Even preaching a moral text requires theological interpretation.

The moral sense often requires looking for a moral even when it is not obvious. For instance, miracle stories obviously point to Jesus' authority and power, yet for example, in the healing of the man who was paralyzed and lowered through the ceiling (Mark 2:1-12), a moral can be discerned: Be as faithful as these four friends of the man, or be more faithful than those in the crowd who will not let him near.

Theological criticism goes even further, for it is not content to leave moral instruction indistinguishable from the laws of this world. Biblical examples and laws need to be assessed in light of basic scriptural truth, and it is by such critical endeavor that they gain their distinctive weight. Preachers can make an important practical move: Instead of preaching a text as a mere moral lesson, they can preach it as a theological lesson capable of bearing truth. Thus we move from what we must do (for example, we must be generous) to how this action relates to God's action (only God in Christ is the perfect Giver). God becomes poor on our accounts. We cannot be poor if we are rich in our relationship with God and our neighbors. If those of us with wealth trusted God more, the poor would not suffer.

One can also argue that individuals in the Bible inescapably represent positive and negative models of behavior and are intended by God to do so, for the church through history uses the Bible as a guide to right living. Further, the church understands from earliest times that biblical texts have a plurality of meanings, though it has rediscovered this only recently. Still today one can use the moral sense as a lens to determine if legitimate moral significance exists in a text. Theological criticism provides some responsible strategies that include preaching Christ, biblical characters, and Paul as moral examples.

Preaching Christ as Moral Example

Preaching Christ as a moral example involves portraying Christ's action with sufficient detail such that it is identified or experienced as exemplary whether or not the preacher intends explicit moral focus. Sometimes the moral is to the side of the text: When Jesus responds to the lepers who call out (Luke 17:12-19), few people claim "Jesus is kind" as a main thrust of the text—more clearly he is the one who has the authority to command healing

103

and restoration to fullness of life. Nonetheless, he responds to the deep-felt needs he sees in ostracized strangers, and his love is not incidental to his present journey to the cross. Moral clues from individual texts can be taken in this manner, generalized, and confirmed in the crucifixion, resurrection, and ascension.

Sometimes a moral is drawn from Jesus' words where he intends a moral, for instance in: the Greatest Commandment (Matt. 22:34-40); the Commissioning of the Disciples (Matt. 28:16-20); the good Samaritan, "Which of these three . . . was the neighbor . . .? Go and do likewise" (Luke 10:36-37); or the prodigal son (Luke 15:11-32). Sometimes a moral is inferred from Jesus' words, even though it is to the side of his intent, for instance about stewardship in the parable of the lost coin (Luke 15:8-10) when joy in heaven over repentance is one main thrust. Sometimes listeners will hear a moral message even when the preacher does not intend one or will opt for a moral interpretation because the preacher's meaning is too abstract or difficult. It is for this reason that Origen conceives of the "flesh" sense of the word as help to those least capable of spiritual interpretation.

Obvious dangers arise from drawing a moral from Christ's example. Without historical criticism we are unable to distinguish between a legitimate ethic implied in Christ's behavior and one that we import to Scripture from our setting and culture; we thereby separate the ethic from the culture and religious setting that helps us understand it. Moreover, if we find a moral in Christ's every action, on what basis do we then deny a moral in awkward texts? Still, even in such texts a moral can be discerned though not one involving direct imitation of Christ: Christ overturning the tables in the Temple (Mark 11:15-19) speaks of the need to avoid defiling the holy; his condemnation of the fig tree out of season (Mark 11:12-14) speaks to the urgent need for change; his command to tear out your own eye rather than sin (Matt. 5:29) speaks against judging others; his bringing of a sword and not peace (Matt. 10:34-36) speaks of full commitment to Christ; his rebuke of his mother (John 2:4) speaks against assuming that our agendas are God's; his delay for two days to respond to Lazarus's illness (John 11:6) speaks to the same thing; his condemnation of all the scribes and Pharisees (Matthew 23) speaks against presuming self-righteousness; his commending of the dishonest steward (Luke 16:1-7) speaks of the need for Christ's followers to be shrewd; and his narrative treatment of the elder son (Luke 15:11-32) is a caution against works righteousness.

A further danger with "Christ is our example" is its inadequacy as a statement of his accomplishment. Christ Jesus does not come into the world to give us better directions, to help us to walk in straighter lines, and to correct our step. He comes to save the world. When we conceive that he is our example to imitate, we may underestimate the power of sin and evil in the world that all of our imitation cannot overcome. Christ is the exemplar of our faith, but he is more than this, he is our Savior who dies to destroy death itself and who gives us the power of his resurrection in our baptism through the Holy Spirit.

Preaching Biblical Characters as Moral Example

The reason we tell biblical stories is to communicate faith and Christian life, and in this, biblical characters serve as either positive or negative moral examples. Some of the stories are appalling as in the story of Lot offering his daughters (Gen. 19:8); David arranging for Uriah's death (2 Sam. 11:14-27); the rape of Tamar (2 Sam. 13:1-14); and other "texts of terror" including many that betray the androcentric and often misogynist tendencies in portions of the Bible. Given the negative manner in which women are so often portrayed in the Bible and in our own society, it is appropriate that much current women's literature retells the biblical stories from the perspective of women and upholds biblical women as role models. These are some of the foremost instances of the Bible being used as moral example today, and many of these are easily employed in the pulpit.

Moral examples from the Bible have the greatest strength when they easily connect with issues of life or faith today, for example: One might find in Adam and Eve the need for humans to observe the limitations God places on humanity (Genesis 3); in the story of the widow and the unjust judge the need for persistence in the face of indifferent or dishonest authorities (Luke 18:1-5); or in the Annunciation the need to trust in God when life changes direction (Luke 1:26-38). Of course many social problems that people face today—unemployment, drug addiction, racism, degradation of the environment, and globalization—are not directly addressed by the Bible, and yet need to be addressed from the pulpit. Further, the biblical way of understanding social problems can seem foreign to us, for we rely upon medicine and social sciences like psychology and sociology to help us understand certain kinds of behavior that the Bible understands morally. (Still today many Christians mistakenly assume that if people had stronger faith, they would not necessarily suffer depression or other forms of mental illness.) However, even with the differences between then and now, biblical people can be developed in the sermon to represent faith struggles at the heart of moral issues today.

Jesus himself does not shy from providing moral instruction or using moral example. The moral sense in the pulpit is necessary, and people look to the preacher to help put life into perspective before the Word of God. A moral sense is also unavoidable, for nearly all of the Bible stories we commonly tell are stories of faith that also have a moral and are preserved for a moral purpose. People draw morals all of the time; whenever a story is told from daily life the thrust so often is the perceived right or wrong action. Sermons heighten moral expectation, for the genre implies to many people that behavior needs correction, and preachers need to be attentive not to be heard to make moral judgments where they are not intended. I remember hearing a sermon on the cleansing of the Temple and several people were convinced by it that the preacher was against all business not just that in God's house. People regularly draw morals as part of the hearing process. They turn to God in prayer to ask for guidance, and it is natural that they expect to hear God speak not least through preaching. The wise preacher intentionally engages moral reflection instead of leaving listeners to infer what they will.

Frederick W. Robertson (1816–1853) often uses biblical characters as examples;[28] his sermons sound almost contemporary because he uses narrative and is interested in character long before the influence of Freudian psychology on the pulpit. His sermon on Solomon, based on Nehemiah 13:26, avoids anthropocentrism; he moves from Solomon's sin to God's loving guidance of Solomon in the midst of all his apostasy.[29] Using biblical characters as moral examples is dangerous if, as preachers, we portray them as sources of hope. No matter how much we admire Ruth, Mary, Ezra, or Paul, they are people like you and me and are not God, therefore they are not the source of our hope. They may inspire us to follow their example, but only by pointing to God acting in and through their lives can listeners hope that God might use them in a similar manner. Perhaps all sermons face this bifocal challenge.

Preaching Paul as Moral Instructor

Paul and the other authors of the epistles need separate attention in part because of their importance for preaching. Preachers often love preaching these texts because of the ease with which they connect to today. Ephesians 2:11-22 says, "So then you are no longer strangers and aliens, but you are citizens with the saints and also members of the household of God" (v. 19); a preacher speaks about the Gentiles as strangers and aliens who are formerly excluded from the household of faith, though they are now one in Christ. Historical criticism helps identify the nature and background of the Ephesus congregation, the significance of the author's terminology, and the place of this verse in the larger unit of the letter. Richard Hays helps us read the various New Testament letters narratively and see them as part of a conversation about the story of the church in the first century.[30]

Theological and homiletical criticism takes the matter further: the preacher might legitimately be led by the text to speak of Christ ("himself as the cornerstone"—Eph. 2:20) as the one who becomes an alien and a stranger for us, and in light of his teachings we might also consider what moral response is required of us toward strangers and aliens. In other words the gospel message makes a moral claim upon us even as it frees us. Although a specific text may not explicitly make this claim, it nonetheless is being drawn from the language and symbols of Scripture in a manner for which preachers receive almost no instruction from biblical studies. To the extent that the literal sense of the biblical text "leads" us, what we say is appropriately conceived not as eisegesis, or even as application, but rather as exegesis for it is what the text "leads out" when employing homiletical criticism. Historical criticism takes the same freedom with texts.

Paul uses moral instruction, almost always in the last portion of his letter, after grace is spoken, but his message cannot be reduced to it. Again, with Paul we need to be faithful to what he says and not use moral instruction as the sum total of his message or the gospel truth. In Romans and elsewhere he formulates his theological message first (e.g., here is our relationship with Christ) and then draws out ethical implications, thus we can often look to earlier sections for his theological thrust.

The Moral Sense and Mission of a Sermon

Sermons are not just to be heard, they are "to equip the saints for the work of ministry, for building up the body of Christ" (Eph. 4:12). In other words, sermons lead people to do things in light of the gospel, to change their lives, to act for others without counting the cost, and to have deeper faith and knowledge. A portion of my own denomination's contemporary statement of faith has a moral clause that many denominations can embrace:

> We are called to be the Church:
> to celebrate God's presence,
> to live with respect in Creation,
> to love and serve others,
> to seek justice and resist evil,
> to proclaim Jesus, crucified and risen,
> our judge and our hope.[31]

Within such a mandate, a preacher can make a suggestion about what might be an appropriate response to the sermon. I call this the mission of the sermon; Henry H. Mitchell speaks of a sermon's "behavioral purpose";[32] Thomas G. Long speaks of a "function statement" that identifies what the preacher "hopes the sermon will create or cause to happen for the hearers."[33] I have discussed in previous books[34] that the mission need not necessarily arise directly out of the text but lie in the direction the text points when a preacher asks for such direction. For instances in which the mission does come from the text, some guidance may be offered.

Preachers use the literal sense to ask of the text, *What is God saying or doing in or behind this text?* Preachers use the moral sense to ask, *What are we as humans to do in light of God's Word?* How do we as preachers give moral guidance or instruction without reducing the sermon's message to *you must, should, and have to*? The problem with such a message is that it is obviously anthropocentric; it implies "It is all up to us" and obviates what God does for us in the death, resurrection, and ascension of Jesus Christ. The only way I know to accomplish a proper sense of human duty held in tension with God's empowerment is to separate trouble and grace in the sermon. To develop trouble in the biblical text and in our world then to develop grace in the biblical text and in our world, one ends up with a four-part, or what I call a four-page, model of a sermon. It is a theological model of a sermon, consistent with theological criticism and the purpose and function of God's Word, even as we have many models of sermons that serve the priorities of historical and homiletical criticism. The "pages" can be arranged in a number of effective ways. In this basic model, page two (trouble in our world) is an excellent place for *must, should, or have to* or whatever manner of moral instruction we might choose. When we return to our world in the grace section of the sermon (page four) we do so having already considered *What is God saying or doing in or behind this text?* This action of grace remains the subject of page four, only now we see and experience the good news in our world. Thus, when the mission is identified (perhaps the same task to which the preacher pointed us on page two), it is now presented not as trouble but as grace, not as *have to* but as *may*, not as a prescription but as a suggestion, no longer as command but as invitation; for now, in going to the place of great need, we do so in the expectation of meeting Christ who has gone ahead of us and in the power of the Holy Spirit through whom all things are possible.

Summary Questions for Homiletical (Moral) Exegesis

1. What does God's action in and behind the text imply concerning our action?
2. Is God's action (in a person of the Trinity) a sign of what we ought to do?
3. What action is suggested for our spiritual lives and our relationship with God?
4. What action is suggested for our community lives and our relationships with our neighbor?

5. What explicit command(s) of God does the text contain?
6. What implicit commands of God does it contain?
7. What explicit worldly commands does it contain (i.e., what human commands conflict with God's Word)?
8. What implicit worldly commands does it contain (i.e., what worldly values stand against God)?
9. Events in the biblical text point to what situations in my church? Concerning the disadvantaged? The sick? The imprisoned? The hungry? The weary? The overworked? The powerful? The rich?
10. Events in the biblical text point to what situations in my city and country?
11. Events in the biblical text point to what situations in the world?
12. What is the "letter that kills" (2 Cor. 3:6) in this text?
13. What is the "spirit that gives life" (2 Cor. 3:6) in this text?
14. What does this text imply about what help we need or may expect from God?
15. Does someone's behavior in the text stand as a model for ours?
16. Does the example of someone's faith stand as a model?
17. Can God be discerned to be working in and through the models we find in the text?
18. Can God who is willing to suffer for humanity be discerned in the text or the situations to which it points?
19. Can God who overturns the suffering of the world be discerned in this text?
20. What difference is made for situations in the text and our world by the fact that Christ is risen for us?
21. What does the fact of the resurrection and ascension say specific to these situations?
22. Have I forced a moral onto the text or legitimately drawn one from it?
23. Have I been anthropocentric in my use of ethics?
24. Have I established that good works are by God's grace?
25. Have I developed the relationship between what we

must do (e.g., be generous) and what God has already done (e.g., God is the Perfect Giver)?

26. In using stories from our world to interpret the text, have I modeled moral behavior?
27. In using stories to interpret the text, have I been inclusive of various groups?
28. Have I allowed contemporary stories to communicate something about God?
29. Have I shown empathy for the worst person named (in the text or our world)?
30. Have I provided an example of something practical to do to improve individual or community faith and life?
31. Have I ensured that the examples I provide serve as invitations to faithful living and not as a new set of laws?
32. Is Christ in this sermon our Savior or merely our example?

CHAPTER EIGHT
The Allegorical Sense in History

Historical criticism provides stability for the biblical text by providing a solid and standard base from which to make other interpretative ventures. It is an essential player in warding off allegory, which flourishes in the absence of historical understanding. Allegory can find what meanings it wants in a text and remove possible agreement on what a text means. This danger is compounded since allegory also seems to dispose of history and threatens the authority of Scripture as a record of God's self-revelation in and through historical events. However, allegory is far more pervasive in the Bible and in the history of biblical interpretation than we are prone to think, and its negative influence cannot be guarded against by simply banning its use. One reason scholars maintain vigilance in their general opposition to allegory, long after the place of historical criticism is secured, is the resilience and resourcefulness of allegory: Weed it out of the flower bed and it appears in the vegetable garden; dissuade a student of using it in exegesis and it appears in a sermon. So fearsome and shameful are its dangers historically, particularly in relation to anti-Semitism; so embarrassing is the church's record, particularly in absurd readings of texts; and so hard-won is its suppression that those of us who teach in seminaries often prefer a state of denial and avoid serious talk about allegory. In effect we spray an intellectual equivalent of weed killer on all of the theological ground in order to prevent allegory from reappearing.

In fact, even if we eradicate allegory completely, we would be the poorer for its loss, for contrary to what we have been taught not all allegory is bad, in the same way that not all ivy is poison. Much of what I call allegory is enormously useful, and we cannot engage in any theological discipline without it. As we will see, we use it every time we comment on the Bible, or every time we establish a substantial comparison between then and now. Even discussion of allegory in relationship to the Bible makes many of us nervous, however, like seeing someone play with matches and gasoline. Perhaps the term "allegory" cannot and should not be rehabilitated: So ingrained is its identification with bad interpretation and so valuable is that identification that we are wise where possible to leave that identification largely intact.

In this chapter we consider allegory and typology in the Bible and throughout history. Much of the allegory we talk about in history is bad allegory. We need the term "allegory"—not the bad practice—to understand our historical background and to establish the continuity between pre-Reformation and post-Reformation preaching to the present day, a continuity that has largely been denied. Allegory is not just dumped at the side of the road when the church wearies of it; we continue to journey with much of it. Allegory becomes the means to make multiple-point comparisons; and even as we discard bad allegory, we need to retain the model as a paradigm for connections we make homiletically between the biblical text, the rest of Scripture, and contemporary situations. Because of the anxiety the term generates, the concluding chapter drafts terms other than allegory for the practice of these connections, such as metaphor and analogy, yet retains the understanding that they nonetheless operate within the family of allegory. This approach helps us appropriate what our ancestors taught about preaching from the whole Bible and using theology to read it. Some of our best efforts can be devoted to identifying and suppressing the kind of allegory that stains Christian history and strains our relationships with our most immediate faith neighbors.

A simple definition of allegory is to say or interpret something in the light of something else. John Dominic Crossan defines it as "a story in figurative language whose several points refer individually and collectively to some other event which is both concealed and revealed in the narration."[1] Some disjunction in the narrative of allegory indicates that it is not intended to be understood at face value as an actual representation of reality. Often biblical allegory as story points to history as though the events described are what matter; but something does not quite fit, thus the search for meaning shifts elsewhere, usually to morality or doctrine. The etymological origin of the word "allegory" implies something "other *(allos)* than what is said" or something "also *(allos)*," in addition to what seems to be said. *Inversio*, the common Latin word for allegory prior to the fourth century, indicates an inversion of meaning, either something different from what is said or something that contradicts the literal meaning of the words. As we struggle to distinguish the worst kind of allegory from other kinds, we keep this idea of inversion in mind: Bad allegorical interpretation inverts what the text is plainly saying and claims for it a meaning that denies its historical footing.

Allegory establishes a set of comparisons between things, people, or events in order to develop an abstract concept, moral, or religious truth. Allegory is more than just analogy and is also more than just metaphor. There is a yes and no to allegorical comparison: Not everything that might represent something between the analogy and analogue is intended to do so. For example, G. R. Evans notes: "In allegory, the thing signifying—an object or being within the natural world such as a lion—is used to suggest something beyond the natural world in which, it is implied, certain of the lion's properties are to be found, in a higher, supernatural way, but nevertheless, recognisably the same properties. The Lion of Judah in his nobleness and regality and courage is Christ; but he is not Christ in being yellow and four-footed."[2]

In its broadest sense, allegory is a way of thought that allows one to speak of the hidden mysteries of life, for things are not as they seem; and in the ancient world, this way of thought is as pervasive as it is distinctive. For Plato, sensory forms in the material world (for example, a table) are representations of eternal truth found in ideal heavenly forms. This notion of a Platonic ideal provides an ideal framework for allegory in Hellenistic thought, for it authorizes twinned layers of meaning—a lower and a higher—with one-to-one correspondence between them. Allegory also provides a means for ancient societies to move from a culture based in mythology to a culture based in logical thought, since allegory commonly moves a story or myth to a concept or proposition, as the early church moved from an Old Testament lesson to a theological claim about Christ. Allegory can be conceived positively as a basis for rational thought since it assumes that things in the world are other than they seem and thereby invites a new way of seeing things "other" than what is evident.

In Hebrew thought, Philo affirms the superiority of spiritual interpretation that opens the meanings God intends in Scripture. This is of particular relevance since the historical sense of Scripture apparently eludes him, leaving him with almost no sense of history as is evident in his comment: "Now probably there was an actual man called Samuel; but we conceive of the Samuel of the scripture, not as a living compound of soul and body, but as a mind which rejoices in the service and worship of God and that only."[3] In Judaism of the first seven centuries, the tradition of *midrash* (commentary) as prophecy and parable depended heavily on allegory. Our ancient ancestors understood there to be hidden meaning in both nature and Scripture; they then read Scripture allegorically in light of experience and read experience allegorically in light of Scripture.[4]

The word "allegory" was used in many ways in the ancient world. It was a way of thinking that allowed for another meaning. It was a type of literature designed to yield higher meaning only to those equipped for the task—the Gnostics frequently used it. It was a specific figure of speech and often a synonym for parable or riddle. Genuine allegory was a form in the Bible such that to read it literally was to distort it: for example, Nathan's story of the rich man who prepares the poor man's lamb for his guests (2 Sam. 12:1-4). Allegory was also a way of reading texts in a nonliteral manner that combined the principle of an inspired interpreter with a process of analogy that is close to free association. It was a dominant form of prophecy; in fact many Old Testament texts were made to serve in a literal capacity as prophecy of the Messiah, for example, the accounts in Matthew of the virgin birth (Matt. 1:23) in Bethlehem (2:5-6) and the flight into Egypt (2:15). Of course, as soon as we get into the question of prophecy in the Bible, the nature of allegory may change. We no longer simply say of the texts that they have some random "other" meaning, rather this "other" meaning (for example, the prediction of Christ) is often genuine. Thus, what we have in the Bible frequently can be defended as good allegory, although most of us would never choose to defend allegory. Many of the texts that the church reads as prophetic of Christ nonetheless depend upon a nonliteral, allegorical reading like Isaiah 53, the slaughter of the innocents (Matt. 2:17-18), or the holy family settling in Nazareth (Matt. 2:23).

Allegory also refers to doctrine or what we now call constructive or systematic theology, and it teaches "what we should believe." Allegory has a number of further uses. Anagogy, the third ancient spiritual sense of Scripture beyond moral and allegory, is the prophetic sense that "shows us where we end our strife." Although this traditional prophetic sense deals with the end times, in practice, allegory often performs its functions. Allegory provides the mechanism to identify Christ as the final future fulfillment of Scripture. Allegory is sometimes used as a synonym for all of the spiritual senses. It can also be a way to avoid the literal sense of a text when its meaning is unclear or unedifying. Allegory is a means to move from a doctrinal truth to a specific biblical text or from a biblical text to a teaching of the church. Allegory is a tool to explore the profound mystery of Christ through exploring the hidden meaning of Old Testament texts. Allegory includes the practice of finding types of the church and of the last things in past and present events. We will consider this latter practice, known as typology, shortly.

Underlying all of these functions for our forebears was the role of allegory as God's means to communicate divine truths embedded in the things, people, and events of the past. Our ancestors understood that nature, history, and Scripture could all be read spiritually to discern hidden meanings that God intended them to find by using the Holy Spirit to guide them. The principle is not too different from our own assumption that poems and many movies are intended to yield a hidden meaning. It also resembles the tendency of contemporary people in Bible study to dispense quickly with the historical background of a biblical text and get on to what it means for today or of many preachers to turn to a text and ask immediately, "How will this preach?" as though the historical gap does not need to be negotiated.

The roots of Christian allegory and its close cousin typology are in the Old Testament and its subsequent Rabbinic tradition. Every detail of the flight from Egypt is understood as prophetic of a type or feature of the Messianic Age to come. As R. P. C. Hanson writes:

> The Rabbis conceived of Israel's redemption in the Messianic Age as foreshadowed in every detail by the redemption from Egypt as its type. As Israel was delivered in one night, so will Israel be delivered in one night in the Messianic times. The days of the

Messiah would be forty years, as Israel was chastened forty years in the Wilderness (this from Rabbi Akiba). As Israel was fed with rich food in the Wilderness, so will God feed them at the Last Time. As God took vengeance on the Egyptians at the Exodus, so will he take vengeance on Edom (Rome) at the Messianic time; he will bring upon them frogs, flies, all sorts of beasts, plague, scab, hail, locusts, darkness; and he will slay their firstborn. Though in Egypt Israel went out in haste, at the Messianic Deliverance she will not go out in haste nor flight, but God will go before her. As the first deliverer (Moses) revealed himself and then hid himself, so will the last deliverer, the Messiah. And the deliverer will lead them out of the land into the wilderness of Judah and cause them again to dwell in tents, and whoever believes in him will remain in life, but whoever does not will go to the nations of the world and they will kill him. At the end God will reveal himself to them and cause manna to come down for them.[5]

This double grid of meaning is basic to early and medieval thought. The fact that each point on the historical grid of Israel corresponds with a detail on the Messianic grid makes this an allegory and not just an analogy. The degree to which Christians overlook the Jewish roots of their allegorical interpretative tradition is apparent in Origen, who preaches on the Old Testament, "If anyone wants to hear and understand these words literally he ought to gather with the Jews rather than with the Christians. But if he wishes to be a Christian and a disciple of Paul, let him hear him saying that 'the Law is spiritual', [and] declaring that these words are 'allegorical' when the law speaks of Abraham and his wife and sons."[6]

Biblical Allegory

Of course both Jews and Christians find instruction and encouragement for their allegorical interpretations within Scripture itself. For early Christians, Old Testament texts seem to have remote historical meaning and their true significance is their revelation of Christ, the church, and the end times. Examples of Old Testament texts that we recognize as good allegory include: the book of Esther; the Song of Solomon (which was read either literally as an erotic love poem or as an allegory about the love of God and the church— Theodore of Mopsuestia cannot live with either and rejects the book); Isaiah 5 (the uprooted vineyard read as an account of Jews and Christians); Isaiah 53 ("like a lamb that is led to the slaughter," understood as a prophecy of Christ's death and the church under persecution); Ezekiel 17:2-10 (the "allegory" or "riddle" of a great eagle that takes the top of a cedar to a new place where a shoot sprouts abundantly); Ezekiel 24:3-13 (the "allegory" of the filthy pot); Daniel 5 (*"mene, mene, tekel, upharsin"* used as a pun on *mina, shekel,* and *two half minas* meaning numbered, weighed, divided, that Daniel uses as a prophecy of the kingdom about to be divided);[7] and Hosea (his marriage to Gomer treated as an allegory of the relationship of God to faithful and unfaithful Israel).

How does allegory work? Already we can observe that allegory makes a comparison between two things: commonly between a story or event and an abstract idea. A distinction is needed between genuine allegory and allegorization, or allegoresis: the former is something the text does and has residing within it, and the latter is something we do to the text when we interpret it using allegorical method. Jon Whitman notes that allegory in antiquity operates by the process of "turning narrative systems into conceptual ones."[8] Allegory makes a comparison of an extended sort that involves at least two points of contact (for instance, Hosea is Israel before God, Gomer is Israel's apostasy). Allegory does not require a one-to-one correspondence with every detail; for example, Hosea's age has no significance in the allegory. Similarly in "Christ is the Lion of Judah" multiple points of comparison are created—that the lion is noble, regal and has courage—each of which corresponds with aspects of Christ's life (we may still choose to call it an extended metaphor). Key details of one event, person, or thing correspond with key elements of another, for example, everything compared with God must be appropriate; thus in the way Gomer is commonly interpreted, her sin prevents her from standing for God. If some major piece does not fit, the allegory collapses.

The New Testament also makes extensive use of allegory, a term that indicates patterns of multipoint comparison and that are to be distinguished from the single-point comparative models of simile, metaphor, analogy, and typology, as we will see. Defining allegory in this way identifies allegory by its basic structure and mode of operation and claims simile, metaphor, analogy, and typology as members of the same family.[9] We will use them as substitute terms but not just yet, for from a technical and descriptive point of view, they do not match the accuracy of the multipoint model of comparison that we may call allegory's web, net, or grid of meaning.

Jesus uses allegory primarily in four ways:

1. He composes allegorically, constructing what he says to appear to have another sense, as in Matthew 13:3-9, the parable of the sower (with the seeds falling in different locations, read as an allegory about faith or the church where he signals this nonliteral or "other" meaning by adding "Let anyone with ears listen"); Luke 10:30-37, the good Samaritan (when not just read morally as instruction to be a good neighbor); Luke 11:5-8, the friend at midnight (an allegory about prayer); Luke 13:6-9, the parable of the barren fig tree (that is given one more year to bear fruit); Luke 14:31-32, the story of the king who plans for war (an allegory about discipleship); Luke 15:11-32, the prodigal son (if read for theological significance); Luke 16:19-31, the rich man and Lazarus (as an allegory of the last judgment); and Luke 16:1-7 the unjust judge (as an allegory about shrewd living).

If Jesus told all of his parables as simple stories and left their religious meanings ambiguous, as above, they would be allegories. However, when he makes his typical reference to, "The kingdom of God is like..." (or some other related phrase, such as Mark 13:33 "you do not know when the time will come. It is like a man going on a journey"), he directs his hearers away from some literal meaning toward an "other" meaning about the kingdom of God that is characteristic of both his situation and his eschatological message. We need not make too fine a distinction between allegory and parable, for the church often assumes that Jesus' genuine allegory is parable. Moreover, parable often functions as allegory, for instance, the parable of the dishonest steward (Luke 16:1-7) when we seek to discern in our own situation who corresponds to the master and steward. Even the addition of a phrase about the kingdom or realm of God signals that it is a parable and cuts short the allegorical search for multiple connections that establish some other meaning. Thus the absence of such a phrase can signal an allegory. Because parables have multiple meanings (in contrast to Adolf Jülicher), they are rich in allegorical potential.

2. As a second way of using allegory, Jesus cites Scripture so as to give it a meaning fulfilled in his time, saying in effect, these

words about the ancient prophet's life in fact also correspond one-to-one with something happening today. Jesus reads Isaiah 61:1-2 and pronounces that it is "fulfilled in your hearing" (Luke 4:16-21). Elsewhere Jesus or the early church says, "For just as Jonah was three days and three nights in the belly of the sea monster, so for three days and three nights the Son of Man will be in the heart of the earth. The people of Nineveh will rise up at the judgment" (Matt. 12:40-41); Jonah is a type of the Son of Man, the sea monster is a type of his death, and the third day is a type of Easter. The cover of this book depicts this pairing of Jonah as a type of Christ; the illustration is actually a medieval Psalter initially taken from Psalm 69, into which this typology was read: "Do not let the flood sweep over me, or the deep swallow me up, or the Pit close its mouth over me" (Ps. 69:15).

3. In his third use of allegory, Jesus sometimes interprets his own words allegorically, or the early church does, explaining what he says so as to indicate plainly the "other" sense he has in mind, as in Matthew 13:36-43 (his allegorical interpretation of the wheat and the tares); Matthew 13:47-50 (the sorting of the various fish from the full fishing net as an allegory of the end times); John 10:1-5 (the sheepfold, the thief, the gatekeeper, and the shepherd's voice as an allegory of life in faith); John 15:1-10 ("my Father is the vinegrower. . . . I am the vine, you are the branches").

4. Jesus' fourth and rarest use of allegory is a hybrid of the previous two approaches: He quotes Scripture to interpret his own narrative composition and to make clear its purpose, as in Matthew 21:42. A phrase from Psalm 118:22-23, "The stone that the builders rejected has become the chief cornerstone," is used to explain his parable of the wicked tenants; thus the tenants stand for the religious authorities, the stone stands for Christ, and his becoming the cornerstone stands for the church. Of course one can interpret Matthew 21:42 to be a simple comparison that speaks of prophetic fulfillment, but the structure is nonetheless multipoint allegory.

Other examples of New Testament allegory indicate how extensive its use is. The Gospel writers, independent of the words of Jesus, use mostly his second manner of allegorical sense, to indicate the fulfillment of the Old Testament promises, for example, in Matthew 2:13-15 (the escape of the holy family to Egypt is seen to fulfill Hosea 11:1, "out of Egypt I have called my son")—in fact

Matthew uses Jesus' life to recapitulate the history of Israel—and Matthew 13:34 (Jesus taught in parables to fulfill Psalm 78:2); in Acts 2:17-21 ("The sun shall be turned to darkness," the fulfillment of Joel 2:28-32) and Acts 2:25-28 (the fulfillment of David's words in Psalm 16:8-11).

Paul uses allegory most commonly to interpret the prophets, for example in: the cluster of Old Testament prophecies he cites in Romans 9–11; 1 Corinthians 10:1-5 ("our ancestors . . . drank from the spiritual rock that . . . was Christ"); 1 Corinthians 10:1-22 (the Exodus narrative is applied to Christians); Galatians 4:21-31 (Hagar and Sarah are the two covenants);[10] Ephesians 5:31-32 (Genesis 2:4 is a "great mystery" that Paul is "applying . . . to Christ and the church"). Paul also composes allegorically, for instance in 1 Corinthians 5:7-8 ("clean out the old yeast [of malice and evil] so that you may be a new batch [of sincerity and truth]") and Ephesians 6:11-17 ("Put on the whole armor of God").

Finally, John's vision in Revelation can be assessed as an extended allegory (even though its significance often eludes us),[11] and in at least two places uses allegory quite specifically: Verse 11:8 portrays Jerusalem "spiritually" (KJV) and "prophetically" (NRSV) as Sodom and Egypt; and 12:1-7 portrays a woman in the desert giving birth to a son as the church that disperses to the nations. The biblical writers seem to make no distinction between the words of the Old Testament that could be understood directly as prophecy and other words that have prophetic significance, for they understand Scripture to be prophecy.

Many of Jesus' parables throughout history are interpreted as allegory before the distinctive design and function of parable is understood; now we seem to be at a place where even his allegories are treated as parables.[12] Given the historical background, there is no reason Jesus would not have used allegory: it was "in the air."

Allegory received substantial encouragement from the founders of the church. However, their allegoresis was of a different order from allegory, for they used it to attach prophetic significance to texts. Early church interpreters and preachers used it to accomplish three things related to Scripture: (1) to know how their own experience of salvation in Jesus Christ through the Holy Spirit relates to the Old Testament witness, (2) to preserve the Old Testament in a manner that speaks of one God, the same God that they know in

Jesus Christ; and (3) to make sense of many passages in the Old Testament that do not seem to make literal sense. Once a strong allegorical tradition is established in relation to the Old Testament, one might wonder why this did not generally extend itself to the New Testament in the same way, such that the Gospels and the epistles were not also interpreted allegorically as having an "other" sense. In fact the Gnostics did move in this direction. The reason the church did not is clear: If early Christians had difficulty discerning or believing the historical events behind the literal sense of the Old Testament, they did not experience this with the New Testament. Moreover, since the Old Testament was fulfilled by the New—a medieval maxim said, "The Law, . . . spiritually [i.e., allegorically] understood, functioned in exactly the same way as the Gospel"[13]—there is no need to seek a further fulfillment, except in the restricted sense of anagogy and the end times.

Allegory, Typology, and Biblical Interpretation

New Testament typology is a close relative of allegory. Typology (not to be confused with tropology, the moral sense) is the study of "types," "figures," or recurrent patterns, such that a person, thing, event, or idea at one time is compared to another on the basis of a single point of comparison and is interpreted to belong to the same genre or to have the same significance as another. In biblical criticism, typology is used like allegory as a means to relate the Old Testament to the New on the basis of an overarching type, the Old Covenant and the New. Following ancient Jewish principles of exegesis, typology compares on the basis of like to like, external to internal, known to unknown, or lesser to greater, for example from the promised land to the kingdom of heaven, always seeking fulfillment in the Christ event, the church, or the end times. Just as no biblical text can have a literal meaning unworthy of God, so too, no typology can be established that will apply anything inappropriate to Christ or the Church.

Biblical scholars like to make the distinction that typology is good and allegory is bad, but in ancient thought there is no distinction: They both demonstrate the unitary action of God throughout salvation history. For example, Paul uses the word type *(typos)* for what seems to us is an allegory (1 Cor. 10:1-12). The early church makes no distinction between typology and allegory, and the beginning of interpretation using types is unclear.[14] R. P. C. Hanson identifies that typology comes to Palestinian Judaism from outside sources.[15] The step is small from Jewish typology to Jewish allegory. For example, the Jewish writer of the ancient Damascas Document (ca. 106–70 B.C.) interprets a contemporary event using the song in Numbers 21:18, and employs several types in his allegorical interpretation:

> "A well the princes digged
> The nobles of the people delved it
> By order of the Lawgiver."
> The well is the Law, and they who digged it are the penitents of
> Israel . . . and the Lawgiver is he who studies the Law. . . .
> And the nobles of the people are those who came to dig the well
> by the precepts in which the Lawgiver ordained that they should
> walk throughout the whole period of wickedness.[16]

Moisés Silva claims that typology is developed within Christianity by the Antiochene school "in conscious opposition to allegorizing" and that it is a method of finding meaning in the literal events of history in the Bible.[17] However, the soil in which allegory and typology thrive is already well tilled before the New Testament is written. When it is set alongside the Old, Christians have further encouragement to develop allegorical connections.

Typology, like allegory, makes a comparison between two times, persons, things, events, or ideas, yet is unlike allegory in that it relies upon only one point of similarity. Other figures of speech more familiar in our day also make a comparison on the basis of one point of similarity: Simile makes comparison using "like" or "as" ("this is like this") and metaphor makes it on the basis of identity ("this is this"). When John the Baptist calls Jesus the Lamb of God (John 1:29), at a strictly literary level he is using a metaphor, saying that Jesus is God's special Lamb because he is God's chosen one. However, more accurately for John (the Baptist and the Gospel writer), Lamb of God evokes memory of the sacrificial lamb at Passover in Egypt, and prophetically anticipates the outcome of Jesus' life on earth. The former event is a type of the latter. Biblical typology follows a temporal trajectory. Typology does not establish an equation between the different ends of the trajectory but assumes the superiority of the latter as the fulfillment of the former, thus Christ is the antitype, or "opposing" type, or the reality to which the type points. Melito of Sardis (ca. 130–ca. 190), in the oldest Christian sermon after Second Clement,[18] "Peri Pascha" (On the Passover), explains his understanding of types using Isaiah 53:7:

> For although *as a sheep he was led to slaughter*,
> yet he was not a sheep;
> although *as a lamb speechless*,
> yet neither was he a lamb.
> For the model indeed existed,
> but then the reality appeared.[19]

Typology is easily expanded into allegory by moving to two points of comparison, and in biblical interpretation such expansion often takes place. As we compare, for example, the narrative associated with the Paschal lamb in Egypt and the narrative grid of Christ's life, an allegory begins to takes shape: Christ died a sacrificial death on behalf of others, and those who are marked by his blood are spared the death that is to come. Each of the various points of allegorical comparison is type and antitype, thus the Passover lamb's death is a type of the crucifixion; the blood of the lamb on the doorposts and lintels is the occasion of death "passing over" and a type of the blood that we drink in communion; and the death visited upon the firstborns in Egypt is a type of the punishment reserved for those who refuse to believe.

The *Revised Common Lectionary* explains the pairing of Gospel and Old Testament readings for the Sundays after Epiphany and Pentecost as typology: "The Old Testament passage is perceived as a parallel, a contrast, or as a type leading to its fulfillment in the gospel."[20] We do not like to think of allegory and typology as related, for we try to keep allegory distant. However, this interplay exists between them, and often in the history of preaching what is identified as allegory is also referred to as typology; and allegory is often considered as the "typical," or normal, sense since it is the theological meaning. Further, as soon as we ourselves explain typology in a sermon, our explanation itself turns into allegory because we open multiple points of comparison.

Examples of New Testament typology include: John 6:49-59 (Jesus is "the living bread . . . from heaven" in contrast to the limited sustenance Israel received, manna in the wilderness); Romans 5:14 ("Adam, who is a type of the one who was to come"); Romans 10:6-10 (Moses' words in Deut. 30:12-14 are a type of justification by faith); 1 Corinthians 10:1-2 (the Red Sea is a type of baptism, and Israel is a type of the Corinthians); 2 Corinthians 3:7-17 (Moses' transfiguration is a type of Christ's); Galatians 3:16 (Abraham is a type of Christ); Ephesians 5:14 (citing Jon. 1:6, Jonah is a type of the awakening sleepers upon whom Christ's light will shine); Hebrews 9:24 (the sanctuary is a type of Christ's heavenly one); Revelation 5:12 (Christ is the Passover lamb); and Revelation 19:13-15 (vengeance on Edom in Isaiah 63:1-6 is a type of Christ's judgment).

Allegory and typology, used as interpretative methods, function diachronically (that is, through time) to establish their comparisons along a line of linear history instead of synchronically (that is, at one point in time) between simultaneous events. One difference between typology and bad allegory (or allegoresis) is that typology makes the comparison yet allows the type to maintain its historical integrity. Bad allegory says the only real meaning is the spiritual one uncovered by its agency.

Allegory and typology can be considered as figures of speech, structures of thought, methods of composition, or means of interpretation, and nothing in this limits them to linear history. In fact the ancient Greeks used typology and allegory in a nontemporal manner in their dramas, where characters regularly wore masks to represent abstract values that roughly corresponded to events in the viewers' lives. Medieval traveling plays like *Everyman* and the *York Cycle* of plays used allegory in the same fashion, and modern medicine diagnoses disease by using atemporal types of symptoms (for instance, a doctor might say, "Your four symptoms correspond to the description of the disease described in this book"). The temporal axis is simply a distinctive feature of allegory and typology in biblical interpretation where events pretype or prefigure others. In other words, biblical allegory and typology find similarities, echoes, and reflections between people, things, events, or ideas at different times in history and read prophetic significance into them. They assume that God uses certain events in Scripture and history as a way to anticipate others, to signal to the faithful what God is doing, to identify when prophecy is fulfilled, and in so doing, to demonstrate God's trustworthiness.

Allegory in History

Some indication needs to be provided here of the allegorical sense through history, although its use is so extensive that a few samples will suffice. When the early church banned allegory it was not opposed to allegory in general, just allegory as a basis for doctrine and allegory that did not lead to the true Christ-meaning of prophecy. Origen treats the Samaritan woman in John 4:28 as an allegory: She abandons the well of false teaching and heresy for the pure doctrine Christ offers.[21] Gregory of Nyssa, in his *On the Life of Moses*, first reconstructs the historical events in Moses' life and then retells his life as an allegory of the soul's ascent to unity with God in Christ (that is, the burning bush, Red Sea, wilderness, manna all have "other" significance). Irenaeus, bishop of Lyon, was irritated with scholars of his own age who claimed that Jesus was silent for thirty years before beginning his ministry and that this prophesied thirty great aeons in the eternal silence of God.[22]

Karlfried Froehlich identifies from the seventh-century "Papyrus Michigan" some lists of standardized allegorical equivalencies for Proverbs and the Gospels of the sort that were used by preachers and teachers and that "reflect longstanding school tradition."[23] For example, concerning Proverbs 13:14:

"The law of the wise is a fountain of life."
The law is the proclamation;
the wise man, Paul;
the fountain of life, Christ.

Concerning John 2:1:

"On the third day there was a marriage at Cana in Galilee."
The day is Christ;
the third, faith;
the wedding, the calling of the Gentiles;
Cana, the church.[24]

Related to this is a twelfth-century form of a dictionary of the senses of Scripture that is designated as a *distinctio*.[25] In it preachers can search for how biblical texts are employed using fourfold exegesis.

Allegoresis in the Middle Ages generally was a way of illustrating theological truths that were already established and not a means of establishing doctrine. Andrew of St. Victor (1110–1175) ventures an allegorical reading of Jeremiah 1:5 in which "Before I formed thee in the bowels of thy mother" actually means "in the synagogue."[26] Stephen Langton (ca. 1300) interprets Joel 2:30 ("The sun shall be turned to darkness and the moon into blood") as a commentary on the need for the church to give its greater light to the state. Medieval figures like Langton did not normally use allegory in their theological arguments but did use them in their glosses on Scripture. When someone objected to his allegorizing as arbitrary and therefore meaningless, he found such complaint irreverent and disrespectful of the Christian faith, for faith was the content of all allegory.[27]

For Aquinas, "the 'allegorical' sense occurs whenever things described in the Old Testament anticipate, independently of their original context, things in the New Testament."[28] Luther's literal sense is christological, and although he speaks against allegory, he continues to court it after he bases his interpretation in the literal. For example, in preaching on the good Samaritan (Luke 10:23-37), for the first half of his sermon he concentrates on the lawyer who offends both God and humanity by his adherence to the law. In the second half he moves to allegorize:

> We will now see what is contained in the parable. The Samaritan, in this place, is without doubt our Lord Jesus Christ, who hath declared his love toward God and man....
>
> This is that Samaritan, who, without being desired by prayers, came and fulfilled the law: he alone hath fulfilled it, which praise none can take from him....
>
> By the Priest, is signified the holy fathers which flourished before Moses: the Levite is a representation of the priesthood of the Old Testament. All of these could do nothing by their works, but passed by like unto this Priest and Levite.[29]

Luther's interpretation of Christ is quite appealing, as allegoresis often can be. From our contemporary perspective, the problem is the claim of allegorical interpretation that the text actually refers to Christ. Most preachers today would have no difficulty if Luther interpreted the parable on its own and subsequently established a simple parallel to Christ (that is, a simile or metaphor) without claiming "the text means this." For Luther, Scripture interprets Scripture based on typology or what one commentator calls the "echo of Scripture within Scripture."[30]

Calvin mocks unidentified ancient authorities who claim of Genesis 18 that Abraham bows once to the three angels and thereby acknowledges that God is one in three.[31] Calvin claims that Adam, Noah, Abraham, and the rest of the patriarchs are genuine believers because they received illumination from the Holy Spirit through the Word and perceived "God not only as Creator but also as Redeemer."[32] Such illumination is stronger than rational proof (7:4) and provides an ongoing basis for allegory; in spite of his protests against it, christological interpretation is for him the true meaning of Old Testament passages. Calvin believed that allegorical interpretation of texts that had a plain meaning was demonic. He nonetheless approved of allegorical interpretation for Old Testament passages that described the church, Christ, the Realm of God, and prophecies that seemed as yet unfulfilled. He made abundant use of typology.[33]

For both Luther and Calvin the Old and New Testaments form an actual unity; they are not merely united in purpose. Luther uses law and gospel as dimensions of God's one Word to articulate this unity and Calvin uses Christology. The Old Testament bears witness to Christ as much as the New Testament, but by a different means: through foreshadowing and types.

For Melanchthon, echoes of Scripture within Scripture are categorized by doctrine arranged according to certain common places or *loci communes*. These are based in allegory and naturally flow from major Christian themes like sin, law, salvation, and grace. Biblical characters are historical people as well as Christian types that allow for connections with individual stories and the entire biblical story since the Bible has a unity and one consistent theme.

Allegoresis keeps reappearing in Christian preaching. One of the most famous examples is Barth's treatment of the prodigal son who is Jesus Christ in going to the "far country" of human sinfulness where he dies and who, in being raised from the dead and ascending and in returning home to God, makes it possible for humans to return home: "It was God who went into the far country, and it is man who returns home. Both took place in the one Jesus Christ."[34]

Allegory is not confined to preaching. Much famous literature is extended allegory: Langland's *Piers Plowman*; Spenser's *Faerie Queen*; Dante's *Divine Comedy*; Bunyan's *Pilgrim's Progress*; Jonathan Swift's a *Tale of a Tub*; Hawthorne's *Scarlet Letter*; Melville's *Moby Dick*; Joyce's *Ulysses*; Chesterton's *Man Who Was Thursday*; C. S. Lewis's *Narnia*; Orwell's *1984*; Kafka's *The Castle* and *The Trial*, and Miller's *Crucible*. Much children's literature is allegory, for instance, the story of the Three Little Pigs is about animals but says something to children about their own lives. Science fiction functions in a similar manner, using a projected future to say something to civilization at present. Many recent movies like *Pulp Fiction, Magnolia*, and *Being John Malkovich* are obvious allegories. Perhaps we should be less surprised at the extent of allegory in our culture than at our reluctance as Christians to recognize it when it is staring us in the face, even in biblical interpretation. Still, our own postmodern age has an ambivalent relationship to authority in general and is bound to find much allegorical interpretation to be too inelegant, too controlling, too indirect a means of communication, too little addressed to the heart, and too much addressed to the head. After working through the allegorical web of "this means this . . . and this means this . . . and this means this," individuals in our age are likely to say, "Who says?"

Allegory and Doctrine

The allegorical sense offers "what you should believe," and it is the doctrinal sense for most of Christian history. How do we reconcile this understanding with the fact that from the time of Irenaeus, the plain literal sense of biblical texts, rather than the allegorical, is the only sense of Scripture on which to base morality, faith, and doctrine?

To answer, we must return to the double-literal sense. The literal sense at the historical-grammatical level for the early and medieval church is not necessarily a reading that makes sense or has revelatory significance. The literal sense that the church honors and observes is the sense that offers theological understanding, and this sense is arrived at, particularly with the Old Testament, using allegory. When the early church banned allegory as a source of doctrine, they did not ban allegory that demonstrated the true Christ-focused meaning of prophecy but rather banned (1) allegory that violated the plain sense of the texts as the church affirmed it through the rule of faith and (2) allegory based on inappropriate typology that did not disclose the central teachings of the faith or that was unworthy of God. They used the Old Testament as a foundation for morality and doctrine where its meanings were confirmed or consistent with those in the New Testament or their own culture and for finding the authentic hidden spiritual meaning of Scripture. As Andrew Louth notes, "*allegoria* is the usual word the Latin Fathers use from the fourth century onwards to characterize the deeper meaning they are seeking in the Scriptures. Some of the Fathers, it is true, attack what they call allegory and its use; but what they attack are the results (particularly the results that Origen came up with) and not a method."[35] Of course, today we attack the method as inappropriate as well. Augustine finds "almost everything" in the Old Testament is figurative or allegorical, including the historical, because for him, it is about Christ.[36] As he says concerning Noah, "we cannot agree with those who receive the bare history, but reject the allegorical interpretation, nor with those who maintain the figurative and not the historical meaning."[37] Of the fullness of the ark he says, "But none but a contentious man can suppose that there was no prefiguring of the church in so manifold and circumstantial a detail."[38] Still, the central teachings of the church are supported by the literal interpretation of many texts in relationship to each other and by repeated and consistent teachings throughout the whole of Scripture.

In patristic interpretative practice, allegory either does or does not conform to the rule of faith. Included in the good kind of allegoresis are (1) interpretations of texts as direct prophecy that have a theological meaning as their only acknowledged literal sense and (2) texts that have ambiguous literal meaning and can nonetheless be rescued using allegory. The latter cannot serve as the basis for doctrine but, nonetheless, often serve in preaching as a kind of "proof," "illustration," "application," or perhaps even rhetorical "embellishment" of a point being made. Positive use of allegory is a means of linking one text with another elsewhere in Scripture, of explaining unclear texts with clear ones, of demonstrating the unity of Scripture as divine intention, and of showing the wisdom of God in so perfectly designing the world that everything has a purpose and fits into a plan. In this way, allegory is the doctrinal sense that provides "types" representing theological themes and doctrinal links between scriptural passages that, in the medieval expression, "show us where our faith is hid" without actually being the basis of doctrine. One element of allegory that is important for our own age to recover for preaching is precisely this kind of interconnectivity among texts so that we can find better ways of proclaiming the gospel message in its fullness. We may call it something else, but allegory nonetheless continues to provide a basic model for comparing the set of meanings of one text with the larger Christian story.

Reconsidering Allegory

There is every need to avoid bad allegorizing and not to repeat the errors of the past that resulted from ignoring or negating the literal-historical sense of the text. At the same time, preaching is not well served by further silence considering how much the church still relies upon some forms of allegory and how it can be used to good purpose to strengthen proclamation.

One result of the frequent failure to discuss allegory is distortion of fact. For example, James D. Smart, Jesup Professor of Biblical Interpretation at Union Seminary in New York, in 1961 claimed that Jesus avoids allegory: "The rabbis made wide use of allegory in drawing forth the meanings they desired from Old Testament passages; Jesus makes no use of allegory and it is remarkably rare in the whole of the New Testament."[39] His argument is that "the truth of the gospel and the life of the kingdom that came into the world with Jesus were wholly new, unknown to mankind before, and unattainable except through him, and yet that they were foreshadowed and their very lineaments depicted with considerable accuracy long before in the Old Testament."[40] "Allegory," he says "is a means of fastening upon a text a meaning that is not actually present,"[41] and since Jesus offers a new meaning, allegory is not employed. For example, in using Old Testament references to the "day of the Lord," to a new Israel, and to the suffering servant, Jesus uses them as stories about his own life.[42] In other words, something is not allegory if it makes a statement of theological truth that the author intends as the real meaning. Smart takes his position to oppose Barth (in other ways Smart is like Barth) and other scholars in his own time who maintain that allegory is unavoidable in the Bible. One can sympathize with Smart's view given how much we like to keep allegory in a cage, yet his case seems equivalent to denying that Jesus is using a metaphor when he says, "I am the true vine" (John 15:1) on the basis that he is speaking the truth.

To deny the role of allegory in interpretative history or its continuing various forms today is futile; rather we must clarify what distinguishes bad from good. Brevard Childs sees allegory in biblical interpretation at least as an early attempt to deal with the unity of God's purpose and the "ontological and soteriological unity" of the two Testaments—matters that remain unresolved in Christian faith.[43] Other recent claims are more startling. Andrew Louth argues that the tradition of allegory offered preaching the drama and "pressure of the Church's experience of Scripture" and without it, sermons have "degenerated into a moral discourse."[44] Frances Young offers three reasons allegorical reading of the Bible is ethical reading: It allows "the text to impinge on the self and/or the world of the present"; it allows associative intertextual links in the Bible to be explored; and it resists the reduction of "God to an item in the world of the biblical text" that characterizes positivist views of language.[45] David C. Steinmetz argues for the "superiority" of medieval exegesis that allows multiple interpretations that meet the needs of the church and do not allow "the question of truth [to] endlessly be deferred."[46]

One further reason for opening again the question of multiple senses is the crisis in the life of the church and the fact that our current best efforts may not be helping students as much as possible with their preaching. Our age is not being as clear as it could be in offering direction to those who follow. Two homiletics professors from Yale Divinity School separately (and some years apart) raise this possibility: Leander E. Keck speaks of a student who complains he could preach better before taking the course:

> I do not know how he preached before; maybe not as well as he thought. What matters is this: If learning about the New Testament, if saying in abstractions what it really meant, made it

more difficult for him to speak its message, something was wrong even if my intentions were good and my interpretation acceptable. In other words, the critical study of the Bible should make it more accessible, not less.[47]

David L. Bartlett similarly laments, "We [preachers] are so scared of allegorizing and psychologizing that we may be afraid of mattering.... We preach as if we were going to be graded by our seminary Bible professors, not as if we wanted to change the lives of our people."[48]

By being more precise about allegory, its various forms, and what to avoid, preachers may be freed to the potential of "good allegory"—a term that sounds to our ears as good Samaritan must have sounded in Jesus' time. We need to defer for the moment the question of whether the term "allegory" is best used, for it is necessary to frame our discussion. Our general reluctance to discuss allegory suggests not only embarrassment and fear but also lack of understanding. Opposition to allegory is so deeply ingrained that before we can reassess it, we must first clarify three main objections to it and later respond to them.

Contemporary Objections to Allegory

1. To our contemporary minds, allegorical interpretation can seem deceptive. The problem is not that allegory has an "other" meaning, for other figures of speech like metaphor also demand a nonliteral reading; but it is that allegory used as an interpretative device with the Bible seems to trash its common sense. Allegory in the hands of our ancestors was often used to say, "Forget the literal meaning, because this spiritual meaning is what counts." The language of allegory has a certain evocative power, which is part of its danger. As Andrew Louth says, "... we feel that there is something dishonest about allegory. If you interpret a text by allegorizing it, you seem to be saying that it means something which it patently does not."[49] David Buttrick is concerned with a theology that uses deceptive strategies: "What's wrong with allegory? . . . The real reason for rejecting allegory is theological. Would a God of love who wants to be known by human children speak in code? Worse, would a God of love who wants to be revealed speak in a code that only a very few in-group people can break?"[50]

2. Allegory is understood to dispense with history. Moisés Silva follows Jean Daniélou[51] and Leonhard Goppelt[52] in claiming that allegory, unlike typology, is "a playing down or even a rejection of historicity."[53] Justo L. González has no difficulty interpreting Isaiah 53:7 ("like a lamb [that is led] to the slaughter, and as a sheep before her shearers is silent") typologically, and finds in it reference to historical events in Isaiah's life, in Jesus' life, and in the church. However, if interpreted allegorically, he says, individual words like "lamb" and "slaughter" assume an abstract meaning, "that true virtue, like a sheep, does not defend itself, but is willing to give of itself to others, as a sheep goes before the shearer in order to give up its wool, which will warm and comfort others."[54] Typology, by contrast, allows history to stand and makes comparisons within it.

3. In the same manner, allegory challenges historical-critical method, thereby destabilizing the biblical text and undermining the authority of Scripture. Silva finds that much recent biblical criticism functions like allegory and offers a form of "application" of the text that must not be confused with the text itself:

> The classic grammatico-historical method of interpretation insists precisely that a clear-cut distinction be maintained between exegesis (the biblical author's intended meaning at the time of writing) and application (the meaning, or significance, to the reader now). That distinction lies at the basis of virtually every interpretive advance made in the past couple of centuries, and we dare not undermine it.
>
> Unfortunately, this is the very point at issue in the contemporary debate: is it really possible to exegete a text without appropriating it into the present? . . . All believers recognize that exegesis should not remain merely an intellectual and antiquarian task: it ought to bear fruit in the present. The contemporary claim, however, is not that exegesis *ought* to be applied but that, in the very nature of the case, is it always applied, that we fool ourselves if we think we can formulate a biblical writer's meaning apart from the significance his writing has for us.[55]

Silva refers to those schools of literary critical thought that challenge the possibility of anything objective in the interpretative process, of any agreement about the meaning of a text, and of any traditional notion of scriptural authority. James Barr similarly finds in contemporary criticism a dangerous tendency to seek another level of meaning, similar to allegory.[56]

Responses to Objections to Allegory

Our purpose in responding to some of these criticisms is not to defend what should not be defended, namely, bad allegory, but is rather to prepare for our discussion of good allegory.

1. The common form of allegory is allegoresis and is truly deceptive, yet allegory has other forms and uses that are not. Allegory is less than straightforward, yet this can be said of many figures of speech. Moreover, Louth notes that even the literal meaning of a text and what the author intends are not straightforward: "It may well be difficult to get at the meaning of a literary passage, it may be impossible to be sure that we have arrived at this meaning: but the idea that the text means what the author meant it to mean—the idea, almost, that the meaning of a text is a past historical event—gives us a sense that the meaning of a text is something objective, something unproblematic."[57] He argues that our understanding of the literal sense is full of "unexamined idealization" and laden with biases we do not question. Moreover, historical criticism assumes the literal sense of Scripture is the historical sense of Scripture, and this needs challenge.

2. The tendency of allegory to deny history is a design flaw that merits a recall not of all models of allegory, just of the old allegorizing models the likes of which Origen drove. Bad allegory as an interpretative device attributes a lesser value to history because it imagines some signal from the biblical text that indicates the presence of an "other" intended sense. This signal is often an ambiguity in biblical language, or in the case of the Old Testament, an allusiveness of the historical sense. In practical terms, the interpreter seeks a conceptual web or grid on the basis of which to understand the meaning of the text. The conceptual grid most commonly is something in the life of Jesus, the theology and faith of the church, or the end times. Nowadays, signals of ambiguity in the biblical text should send us to historical and literary criticism for answers.

3. Historical-critical method serves as a platform for any reconsideration of allegory for preaching. Historical criticism is not objective, and we can never use it to claim the final word on what a text means, for we are always limited by our inability to escape the present. The text will mean something different in other ages.

Nonetheless, historical criticism provides the best normative standard we can hope for in biblical interpretation, and all other methods of interpretation depend on it. We cannot side with those who argue for "free" interpretation of the sort that allows individuals or congregations to find whatever they want in Scripture in order to justify their own positions. To explore allegory for homiletical potential thus implies embracing historical criticism, not rejecting it. Nonetheless, historical and literary criticisms still need to be placed alongside theological and homiletical criticisms in a parallel relationship of mutual dependence that, far from diminishing one or the other, provides the only way to utilize the potential of each for proclamation.

CHAPTER NINE

Allegory, Anagogy, and Preaching

In this practical chapter we examine two spiritual senses—allegory and anagogy—to determine good uses they have as preaching lenses today. This much is obvious: Preachers ought not to engage allegory as a compositional method, creating an allegory of the naïve sort, which turns the sermon into one long extended allegorical story that says one thing and means quite another. Even if a person of exceptional talent is able to pull this off, from a pastoral perspective it still keeps hearers at arm's length. The attention of the preacher is appropriately directed to hearing and interpreting the Bible as Scripture with a view to hearing what God is saying and making this clear today, not with a view to seeing how clever a preacher can be with a form that is often awkward in our hands and time.

Allegory cannot be employed as an interpretative method that denies the literal-historical sense. Some preachers still do this, as David E. Reid discovered when he visited a church and heard an allegorizing sermon based on the homiletically "unpromising" brief narrative in Genesis 24:63-64:

> The preacher explained that Isaac symbolized Christ; Rebekah, the church; and the camel, whose physical characteristics would be the focus of his message, represented the grace of God. Then he delivered a seven-point exposition based on an allegorical interpretation as classic as any I've ever heard.
> The camel's nose, he said, can detect water from far away and lead its rider to drink. The spiritual lesson, he added, is that God's grace can lead us to spiritual water. He similarly interpreted and applied six more of the camel's characteristics, none of which was mentioned in the text.[1]

Such preaching sweeps both the biblical narrative and history into the trash bin in favor of the superior insight of the preacher.

What then is left? To what ends can allegory reasonably and significantly be reconsidered for preaching in our time—even if we need to find another name for it? The following are worthy possibilities for allegory: as a paradigm of biblical interpretation; as metaphor and metonymy; as a link to and from our world; as a link to and from other scriptural texts; as a doctrinal grid; and as anagogy to speak of the end times.

Allegory as a Paradigm of Biblical Interpretation

Biblical preachers strive to understand accurately the significance of a biblical text in its original setting and context, to discern what God is saying in and through it, to present in the sermon an image of the biblical text appropriate to its meaning, and to discern the practical implications of that meaning in contemporary life. To speak of this process as exegesis (or exposition) and application, as the church has done for hundreds of years, is convenient and has pedagogical merit because it is both descriptive of many sermons and simple, yet it is too simple as a description of hermeneutical process today. It points to a hermeneutic based exclusively in the "then and now" of history, when often today literary rhetorical analysis provides textual understanding in a more direct way, based in the text and our situation in the present. Further, it implies a homiletic conceived as separate from interpretation that is attached at the end of exegesis where it sits for some as a kind of method for popularizing a message. Still, text and application have the advantage of holding up the beginning and end points of homiletical criticism and of highlighting what is essentially a movement from what the text is saying (that is, the God sense) to what it means (that is, God's action today). In other words, at some point in our sermons, we need to be saying "that means this," making comparisons between our understanding of the text, and now, allowing the relevance that is inherent in the Word to be as fully apparent to the congregation as we are able.

Our model for making such comparison is commonly analogy, or more precisely, simile ("this is like this") and metaphor ("this is that"). We say, for instance, "We are like the disciples," or "We are the Pharisees." Were we to try to make several comparisons at once—"We are like the disciples, the Pharisees, and Jesus"—the distinctive features of each would be blurred and meaningful communication would break down. We necessarily focus on one person, relationship, action, image, or idea in the text; and we transfer or transpose its significance into our time. This much is generally agreed upon in homiletics, and for this reason metaphor, simile, analogy, or typology are the bases for our making simple homiletical connections between the Bible and now.

In order to make these connections, preachers do not engage in some wild exercise of the imagination. We must first see what a text is actually saying. I teach students to state each idea in a biblical text as a complete sentence and to list these as concerns of the text. A concern of the text is any idea with which a text is authentically concerned, and it may be derived from the words of the text, from commentaries, or from relevant background, historical or theological, information. It is expressed in a sentence as short as possible in order to confine it to one thought. Each concern becomes a potential point of contact with our own situation. In Luke 7:36-50 the sinful woman is forgiven by Jesus at the house of Simon the Pharisee. A number of concerns of the text are possible points of contact: She is a sinner; She is repentant; She knows her Savior; She is forgiven; She is forgiven much; She accepts her forgiveness; She is indebted to Jesus; She is grateful to him; She shows him great love; She gives him a costly gift; She gives him herself. She is not like many in the church on a range of points as well: She is totally devoted to Jesus; She is totally focused on him; She kisses his feet; She is an uninvited guest to his table; She has no value in her society; She does not care what others think of her actions.

This is where the model of a single point of comparison breaks down, however; for in sermon composition, an analogy must not only be appropriate, it must also be appropriately represented in the sermon and effectively communicated. This cannot be established by looking at just one idea in the biblical text. To confine comparison between the Bible and today to one point is almost impossible; we draw on a set of comparisons and make several analogies. One point of comparison says very little: The woman is uninvited. More needs to be said in the sermon to establish a valid analogy with the congregation: She was the victim of prejudice; She was a sinner; She repented; She sought forgiveness. Further, contrasts need to be drawn that are negative points of comparison to explain the historical and cultural difference between her situation and ours: Simon is an established member of society; women do not eat with the men; guests lie down with their feet away from the table; provided there was room, uninvited guests are allowed to stand around the edge of the chamber in silence and to overhear the conversation. The purpose of historical criticism is to help the reader to negotiate precisely this kind of cultural gulf that exists between the text and now. What may seem like one analogy (i.e., We are like the sinful woman) becomes a range of analogies.

For this reason a single point comparative model is inadequate to describe what actually takes place. Metaphor and simile are the terms I prefer, yet they are inferior paradigms for this relationship because their one-on-one comparative structure does not allow for the complex web of connections between the text and today.[2] We can speak of extended metaphor (or extended simile) without any obvious gain in conceptual clarity, and there are other candidates to explore.[3] Analogy is a possible candidate for this paradigm that has some practical as well as historical advantage. My friend and colleague Stephen Farris uses it to discuss how the Bible connects with our lives, and he demonstrates how to find potential analogies with individuals, groups, or God in biblical texts.[4] Historically, the analogy of Scripture *(analogia Scriptura)* is the practice of interpreting unclear passages with clear ones on the same subject or theme, and the analogy of faith *(analogia fides)* is a more precise form of it, offering a general theological explanation of an ambiguous text. Analogy is a convenient term to use, yet in its ancient form of *analogia Scriptura*, who is to say what text is clearer than another or that two texts thematically are the same? Analogy is even less precise than metaphor in describing how meaning is generated and suffers the same single-point limitations.

Allegory remains the most effective multipoint comparative paradigm for biblical interpretation. It assumes a one-to-one correspondence between two grids on which there are at minimum two places of contact yet does not require all things to correspond. At individual places of contact, simile, metaphor, analogy, and typology still function. This paradigm does not imply a new practice, it simply best identifies what we already practice. In fact, allegory is a paradigm for all interpretation. Literary critic Northrop Frye once commented on poetry, "It is not often realized that all commentary is allegorical interpretation, an attaching of ideas to the structure of poetic imagery. The instant that any critic permits himself to make a genuine comment about a poem (e.g., 'In *Hamlet* Shakespeare appears to be portraying the tragedy of irresolution') he has begun to allegorize."[5] Note that his comparison is not to an isolated detail of the text but to a complexity of details and actions in plot, characterization, and staging that form a grid of meaning. Biblical commentators as well as preachers make this kind of move all of the time, attaching ideas to narrative and other structures in the biblical text and saying "this means this." Frances Young says, "Every critical reading shares something with allegory; every attempt at entering the world of the text, or seeing the text as mirroring our world and reflecting it back to us, involves some degree of allegory."[6] Jon Whitman adds:

> It can be argued, for example, that any composition may have some "other" sense. . . . Perhaps the dominant attitude in current classifications is that there are degrees of allegorical composition, depending on the extent to which a text displays two divided tendencies. One tendency is for the elements of the text to exhibit a certain fictional autonomy. The other tendency is for these elements to imply another set of actions, circumstances, or principles, whether found in another text or perceived at large. The story of a journey, for example, may develop into an a[llegory] of the Exodus by its evocation of a wilderness and a promised land. The extent of such an a[llegory] diminishes, however, insofar as the "journey" is either reduced to a short-lived figure of speech or elaborated into an explicit paraphrase of the biblical account itself. . . .
>
> . . . Recent crit[icism] sometimes applies the term to all interp[retation], viewed as the reformulation of a text into other terminology.[7]

One reason allegory is currently applied in this broader fashion is that Aristotle's notion of semantic equivalence in language has broken down: Text and interpretation are no longer seen to share the same identity.[8] Thus, when we consider an interpretation of a text we are not seeing the text in disguise; Aristotle implies that a text in other words is still the same text. Rather, we have two distinct texts that correspond to each other in many respects. The new comparative model is needed to describe their complex interaction. It is ironic that five hundred years after the church showed allegory the exit door it is back in the pulpit—albeit in a far different form that bears little resemblance to its former self, and now as a paradigm for biblical interpretation.

Allegory is too important to preaching for it ever to disappear. It helps us appreciate the complexity of our homiletical task. Still, the term "allegory" is like a dangerous offender out on parole: It has such recidivist tendencies that we are wise not to free it beyond the paradigmatic level. I propose, therefore, to speak of allegory, first, as metaphor (in spite of the deficiencies of this term) to discuss specific links preachers make between the biblical text and our situation; and, second, as analogy (in spite of the deficiencies of this term), using it in one of its forms throughout history, to discuss links preachers make between biblical texts.

Allegory as Metaphor: A Link to and from Our Situation

Metaphor is a helpful term to establish how a biblical text links with people today; people hear these links in the sermon as metaphors of their own lives. Throughout history, metaphor and allegory are understood to be intimately related: As Calvin said, "allegory is only a continued metaphor."[9] Metaphor has a two-part structure: It makes a comparison saying "this is that" (or in the case of its lesser relative, simile, "this is like that"). For preachers, one part of the metaphor is established with a concern of the text, which is any idea with which the text is concerned stated in a short sentence. The other part is established with a concern of the sermon, which is a transposed version of the concern of the text using a short sentence in which one term is changed. I explain this process in a previous book,[10] but Luke 7:36-50 serves to demonstrate:

Concern of the Text	Concern of the Sermon
The woman is a sinner.	We (or many) are sinners.
She has no societal value.	Many people are given no value.
She is an uninvited guest.	Many are excluded.
She is repentant.	We would like to repent.
She knows her Savior.	We know our Savior. (or: many do not)

She shows him great love.	We do not (or: would like to) show Jesus great love.
Jesus receives her love.	Jesus receives our love.
Jesus forgives her.	Jesus forgives us.
Simon complains of Jesus' favor.	Many complain at God's grace to others.
She is forgiven much.	We are forgiven much.
Jesus gives her a costly gift.	Jesus gives us a costly gift.
She accepts her forgiveness.	We do not accept our forgiveness.
She is indebted to Jesus.	We owe Jesus our lives.
She gives him a costly gift.	We are reluctant to give of ourselves.
She is totally focused on Jesus.	We long to be totally focused on Christ.
She does not care what others think.	We long not to care what others think of us.

Lining out the pairs in this fashion allows the preacher to select only the best for sermonic development. A four-page model of sermon might flow like this: page one (a concern of the text): The woman is a sinner. Page two (a concern of the sermon): We are sinners. Page three (the major concern of the text): Jesus gives her a costly gift. Page four (the major concern of the sermon): Jesus gives us a costly gift. In composing the pages under the guidance of these sentences, other concerns of the text need to be utilized, thus further comparisons are established or implied. Each paired unit of concerns functions typologically as an initial point of contact between the text and our world, rather like the initial strand a spider uses to bridge two branches—the spider then spins an entire web of connections.

Not any transposition will do. Homiletical criticism, even at this primitive stage of sermonic exploration, helps shape our sentences and establish metaphors that make worthy comparisons. For example, when I transpose "She is repentant," I do not choose, with my own congregation in mind, "We are repentant," because, as a congregation, we may need help in seeking repentance; instead I choose "We would like to repent," which I can claim more readily. In another congregation, I might choose, "We would rather not repent."

Application implies a one-way process that happens at the close of exegesis, much in the manner that people once spoke of moving from what a text "meant" in its own time and place to what it "means" today[11]—a model in which texts stand as independent units that yield their meaning in a neutral manner to objective readers, somewhat like cows yielding milk to a machine. Homiletical criticism, however, happens not after biblical exegesis is complete but throughout the entire homiletical and interpretative process, though at any one moment we may concentrate on history, theology, or homiletical and congregational issues. Interpretation continues throughout. The biblical text never ceases to be involved as the Holy Spirit "leads" the preacher to the text's meaning for the community of faith.

Once a bridge is established between a concern of the text and a concern of the sermon, the preacher uses it like a type to transport the biblical witness into the present community. Interpretation is an interactive venture, however, and meaning significantly flows two ways across this bridge. For example, we might venture "Jesus forgives her/Jesus forgives us" and upon critical reflection improve it to read "Jesus gives her a costly gift/Jesus gives us a costly gift": Historical criticism tells us that the woman's gift is costly (we do not need to go to the version in John 12 for this) for she gives Jesus the ointment, her life, love, and gratitude; and she does not count the cost of Simon's disdain. Theological criticism causes us to ask the cost of Jesus' gift of forgiveness in return, and immediately we are led to the cross. The text does not say this, but theological criticism rightly reads any text in light of the entire gospel. As Farris says, "The context of any particular text is the canon as a whole, of which the life, death, and resurrection of Jesus Christ are the center for Christians. Moreover, we do not come to any text in that canon alone; we come as those who are *in* Jesus Christ."[12] This meaning that connects to the entire gospel is legitimately found in Luke as opposed to being outside it.

Making these kinds of connections between a text and various places on the grid of Christian narrative and meaning is good use of allegory. What distinguishes this from bad use of allegory? Barth's treatment of the prodigal son as Jesus Christ is a bad use of allegory, though it has appeal. Barth knows, better than we, the danger of allegory, yet listen to him wrestle with whether he is using exegesis or eisegesis as he interprets the elder son to be Israel who excludes himself from the Messianic feast:

> There is no explicit mention of this relationship to the Gentiles in the text. But is it not there...? Was it not definitely in the mind of the third Evangelist with his very pronounced universalistic interest? Is it really read into the text? Is it not the case that we cannot really expound the text without taking it into consideration—not in direct exegesis, because it is not there—but in and with and under what is said directly? Do we not fail to do full justice to the passage if we ignore this relationship?[13]

Perhaps Barth can be defended on the basis of Luke 15:1, in which tax collectors and sinners are gathered to hear this parable. If not, the problem with Barth's interpretation is that he can be heard to say what bad allegory says, "You thought the text was about this, but really it is about this other subject." The structure of Jesus' parable is inherently allegorical; thus, no matter how hard we resist allegory, no matter how sophisticated our historical-critical study, and no matter how successful we are in treating the text in its narrative wholeness (that is, at a mainly literary level), we cannot escape some theological significance of the story. We therefore inevitably seek a connection between the father and God.

Bad allegory can be avoided if we stay in the narrative and place the interpretative emphasis on the joy of the father (not God) that "this son of mine [not Jesus] was dead and is alive again" (Luke 15:24, cf. v. 32). Once we have this authentic meaning, we can take an additional trip across the bridge to establish a metaphor or simile: The prodigal is like Christ, for God in Christ comes to a far country and dies. We thus avoid saying that the text is actually about Christ, yet we use the text to access the larger Christian story. We can enjoy this borrowed light for what it is, not the historical meaning and not the legitimate God sense but an individual comparison to which the text leads and that stands on its own to make a theological statement. Thus, we can say that the father is like God.

Such journeys across the hermeneutical bridge are not limited to theological criticism—homiletical criticism may use insights from our contemporary situations to determine who in our own society is represented by each son (for example, the younger son represents all sinful living, and the elder son represents the self-righteous). Creative, fresh interpretations of biblical texts often arise in this manner. This happens frequently in the best African American sermons in which preachers affirm the historical meaning of the text as well as the contemporary nature of the story as the community's own. David Bartlett explains:

> In black churches, people would sing and hear "Go Down, Moses." Moses and the exodus were not only "over there" and "back then," they were "here and now." Pharaoh and Mrs. Pharaoh looked a lot like the lord and lady of the house. Martin Luther King, Jr., making his last testament, stood on the mountain and looked over into Canaan. He knew he was not Moses, and he knew he was.[14]

This yes and no of metaphor is powerfully located on the web of unstated allegory.

Two further examples of creative interpretation help to indicate the nature of homiletical imagination, the first from Lancelot Andrewes (1555–1642), one of the best preachers of his day. In an Easter sermon on Matthew 12:39-40 ("Just as Jonah was three days. . . .") that makes extensive use of bad allegory, there is this delightful passage that gives a legitimate twist to our common understanding of Jonah in the belly of the whale:

> There he was, but took no hurt there. 1. As safe, nay more safe there than in the best ship of Tarshish; no flaw of weather, no foul sea could trouble him there. 2. As safe, and as safely carried to land; the ship could have done no more. So that upon the matter he did but change his *vehiculum*, shifted but from one vessel to another; went on his way still. 3. On he went, as well, nay better than the ship would have carried him. Went into the ship—the ship carried him wrong, out of his way clean, to Tarsish-ward. Went into the whale, and the whale carried him right, landed him on the next shore to Ninevah, whither in truth he was bound, and where his errand lay. 4. And all the while at good ease as in a cell or study, for there he indited a Psalm [Jonah 2:2-9] expressing in it his certain hope of getting forth again. So as in effect, where he seemed to be most in danger, he was in the greatest safety. Thus can God work.[15]

We can make a similar venture if preaching on the widow's mite (Mark 12:41-44), bringing to the text an understanding of her situation in faith. We might say:

> How is that widow who is so poor able to give everything she has? She has only two small copper coins, and she stands in line with her meager offering. She has no one with her. She has to come alone. In front of her and behind her are rich men in fine gowns and headscarves of finest blue linen, and she herself is dressed shabbily by comparison. When they step up to give their money, the clanking sound of their heavy coins in the metal pot is heard above the din of the temple crowd. She knows that when she steps up, no one will hear her coins fall. Yet she goes forward to give all that she has. Why does she do that? How can she? She can only do it because she knows her God and trusts in God completely, each day sufficient unto itself. She gives away her coins to help the poor. God still provides for her needs. She knows that. She has that much faith. She has not lived this long without knowing God's love. She is able to give away all that she has because God empowers her. Every morning she gets up and sings her favorite hymns, like "How Great Thou Art" and "Guide Me, O Thou Great Jehovah." Every evening she recites her favorite Bible passages before she goes to bed, like "The Lord is my shepherd, I shall not want." She gives away everything she has because she is willing to suffer, perhaps even to die, for her neighbor. Where did she get a notion like that? Perhaps from the one person in the temple who hears her tiny coins fall.

Preachers receive almost no encouragement or training in dealing with biblical texts in this way from their professors, and it is because for too long we have assumed that the fruits of historical criticism alone can preach. Excellent preaching requires integration of all three kinds of criticism and their accompanying expressions of imagination—historical, theological, and homiletical—and our commitment to their development.

Allegory as Analogy and Typology:
Link with Other Scriptural Texts

Use of the analogy of Scripture *(analogia Scriptura)* is common in the early and medieval church to interpret texts when the historical sense is elusive, and the principle is still of use as a means of reading one text in the light of another and seeing the connections between them. David L. Bartlett provides an extensive and very helpful discussion of how preachers can find models in the Bible for how Scripture interprets Scripture.[16] When two texts are linked by a single theme, echo, type, or reference to the other, analogy is employed, and comparison is established.

Preaching on the Bible as a whole is a hermeneutical principle that dates at least as far back as Iranaeus and is restated for our time by Robert Jenson: "Scripture is a whole. None of its constituent documents or traditions or pericopes or redactions is to be read in isolation from any other.... [T]he canonically shaped Bible is the unitary object of interpretation."[17] Here we speak primarily of secondary scriptural reference in the sermon and of ways in which a preacher might move from a primary text to the larger story. Sandra M. Schneiders identifies such use of texts as accommodation: "The biblical text has always been used in a so-called accommodated sense in the homiletic and pastoral tradition of the Church, and often enough in its theological tradition. Accommodation refers to the use of a text independently of its *con*-text. Thus, by definition, accommodated meaning is not textual meaning."[18]

Schneiders is too strict in denying an authentic contextual meaning in an accommodated text, for some texts used in this way carry with them their authentic meaning. She identifies two criteria for judging the validity of an accommodated interpretation of a text: "The first is whether the text *can legitimately be removed* from its original context without distorting its sense or destroying its reference; the second is whether the new context into which it is inserted is *susceptible of receiving* it and being illuminated by it."[19] She cites John 8:31-32 as a text that can be used in this fashion: "If you continue in my word, you are truly my disciples; and you will know the truth, and the truth will make you free." Many Psalm or Epistle texts that seem to have little recoverable historical background also lend themselves to her criteria. Any developed concern of the text can lead to similar meaning today and has legitimate claims as a text's meaning.

Secondary texts, those we simply allude to for purposes of quick reference to reinforce an idea or to provide an additional example, ought not to be developed at length in the sermon, and care is needed that they merely season and do not overpower it. Such texts are best handled at face value within certain limits imposed by the rule of faith, thus they are particularly apt and stand with little or no commentary; otherwise, they can become a distraction. They provide reference to the faith at large and often are texts that are well-known and loved. Their recital serves a pastoral purpose. Sidney Greidanus speaks of how such intertextual connections facilitate preaching Christ from the Old Testament.[20] Here are some basic ways in which preachers might use analogy for homiletical purpose.

First, supplementary texts can provide incidental information: Pilate's "Are you the King of the Jews?" (John 18:33) might spark some brief aside on 2 Samuel 7, the oracle that gives a covenant to David and his ancestors. The preacher alternatively might say:

> Jesus can respond to Pilate's question in a variety of ways. He can answer Pilate with the question he asks the man by the pool of Bethesda, "Do you want to be made well?" (John 5:6). He can answer Pilate with the words he speaks to the woman at the well, "The water that I will give will become . . . a spring of water gushing up to eternal life" (John 4:14). He can just say, "I am the light of the world" (John 8:12). He can say anything, but all he says is this: "Do you ask this on your own, or did others tell you about me?"

Second, these texts also serve as examples or illustrations in place of a contemporary example, for instance, if a preacher on the New Testament upholds Ruth as an example of personal dedication.

Third, secondary texts can serve rhetorical effect to develop a point as in this example from Augustine which makes allusion to many texts and types:

> My mouth will speak of the praise of the Lord. . . . He is great as the Day of the angels, small in the day of men; the Word God before

all time, the Word made flesh at a suitable time. Maker of the sun, He is made under the sun. Disposer of all ages in the bosom of the Father, He consecrates this day in the womb of His mother; in Him He remains, from her He goes forth. Creator of heaven and earth, He was born on earth under heaven. Unspeakably wise, He is wisely speechless; filling the world, He lies in a manger; Ruler of the stars, He nurses at his mother's bosom.[21]

Fourth, secondary texts can develop hope in a biblical text where it may be understated and need special emphasis. For example, on the expulsion from Eden (Genesis 3), one can preach a conversation of God with Eve that employs a medley of quotations from different places in Scripture

"Eve, there is no turning back to a simpler life," God says in words God also addresses to you and me when we have messed up, "You are leaving Eden, but you are not leaving my love. Where can you go from my spirit? Or where can you flee from my presence? . . . If you take the wings of the morning and settle at the farthest limits of the sea, even there my hand shall lead you. I am not finished with you. You may have messed up, but I still have purposes for you. My forgiveness is from everlasting to everlasting. There is no wrong that you have done that I cannot work for good, for those who love me. I come that you might have life and have it abundantly. And here are some clothes you may wear to keep you warm."

Fifth, one can use the analogy of Scripture to answer difficult questions in one's own text to support the case one is making. For example, why did Job not renounce God as Satan had planned and hoped? A preacher might venture this response:

Job might have renounced God, but in spite of all the suffering that had been visited upon his head—the death of his children, the loss of his wealth, the relentless hounding of his friends who blame him for his losses—he still remembers lessons he had been taught since Sunday school that he still treasures in his heart: He recalls that Noah and his wife kept their faith in God, building an ark when all the land was dry and while neighbors scorned them. They kept faith, too, while they floated on that flood for forty days with the memory that all their neighbors drowned. He recalls how Abraham and Sarah kept faith in God, though their only son Isaac was facing death. He remembers, too, how Moses and Miriam never gave up on God though they wandered forty years in the wilderness. But that is not all Job recalls: He remembers not only the faith of our ancestors, but the faithfulness of God. Job simply cannot renounce God because deep in his heart and without any obvious evidence, he still knows deep down in the marrow of his bones, God has not renounced him.

Preachers can also be more intentional in linking a sermon not just to a specific text but to specific metanarratives of the faith, large stories within the Bible that have the ability on their own to communicate some fullness of the faith. This is particularly important in the relationship to the life, death, and resurrection of Jesus Christ. If we are preaching from the Old Testament, these three metanarratives that Marcus Borg calls macrostories are central: the Exodus, the exile and return, and the Priestly temple sacrifice. He links these typologically with Gustaf Aulen's three images of Jesus: Christus Victor (exodus); Christ as sacrifice (priestly sacrifice); and Christ as revealer (saved from exile).[22] These latter three, of course, allow one to speak in different narrative ways of the cross and resurrection in relationship to most texts. If preaching on the loss of innocence in the Garden of Eden, one can recall that though there is no going back to innocence, Christ in faith gives it back. Most New Testament texts can serve as lenses with which to view the cross, depending on how they are cut, just as many can serve to provide types of Christ.

Secondary use of Scripture comes very close to a devotional use of the Bible that leaves some of us feeling uncomfortable precisely because it bypasses historical meaning. Consider the ambivalence Moisés Silva expresses, at once lamenting, deriding, and resigning himself to allegorical use of Scripture:

[A]llegorical interpretations are very difficult to avoid for a believer who wishes to apply the truth of Scripture to his or her life. . . .
. . . [I]t is unnecessary to point out that every hour of every day

thousands of Christians allegorize the Scriptures as they seek to find spiritual guidance. Moreover, many of the most effective preachers the Christian church has seen made consistent use of this approach. Charles Spurgeon . . . is one of the clearest examples.

None of this makes the method right, and it certainly would be wrong-headed to suggest that allegorical interpretation be rehabilitated in modern scholarship. On the other hand, we can hardly justify developing a hermeneutical approach that works in splendid isolation from the way believers usually read the Scriptures. And the force of this consideration is pressed upon us when we realize that the method played a significant role in the shaping of Christian theology.[23]

Our uneasiness has less to do with a devotional or pastoral use of Scripture in private than with the fear that this type of ahistorical textual use might take over in the public pulpit, as it has in some places already. However, most preachers and pastors know the difference between historical-critical use of Scripture, which God uses to instruct and edify the community of faith, and Scripture used in its pastoral mode, which Christians employ to heal the sick and comfort the brokenhearted. Devotional use of secondary texts in a sermon, in fact, poses less danger than preaching primary texts from only a historical perspective. At funerals, the more faithful pastor is probably the one who takes "in my Father's house are many rooms" at face value rather than insisting that the familiar text is a poor translation. Although not the norm, it is legitimate at times to read Scripture with a view to encountering a familiar word. What is new in God's revelation is always in tension with what is familiar, known, and trusted.

We need to find a way of affirming secondary textual use, not just bemoaning it. The Reformation affirmed the right of all Christians to read the Scriptures for themselves, and the scholarly approach that is essential for preaching and guiding public worship cannot be the only way of reading the Bible. It is the only basis for doctrine and morality, but it is not the only correct way.

Allegory as a Doctrinal Grid

Nearly every time we proclaim God's Word, something of the larger Christian story and the central tenets of the faith needs to be brought into focus. We do not preach a text; we preach God and the faith. We do not preach a small aspect of the faith; we preach something that has the flavor of the entire gospel message. The absence of this expansive message from much preaching leads Edward Farley to challenge preachers to move beyond the preaching of biblical passages and to preach on biblical stories, symbols, social realities, comparisons, moral insight, and editorial slants.[24] Farley laments both the narrow focus on some biblical texts and the nontheological focus of much historical-critical preaching. Two primary factors have contributed to this narrowness: Sermons in our age are shorter than in previous centuries—Jonathan Edwards and John Wesley often preached for over two hours—and our sermons are based on complete units of Scripture instead of a doctrine found in a verse and then expounded from anywhere in Scripture.

Theological criticism, together with the working of the Holy Spirit, allows a biblical text to be received as revelatory.[25] The theological grid we bring to texts is not separate from the biblical narrative grid out of which it arises, and key doctrines (like sin and redemption) often retain an element of narrative plot. Doctrines are teachings of the church grouped into certain themes, which function to identify what aspect of Christian understanding a biblical text best addresses. Robert Jenson describes the kind of theological questioning he brings to a parable:

> Scripture *is* a whole because and only because it is one long *narrative* . . . telling . . . a single story. Therefore, for example, the single most important task of the preacher working on a parable-text is to ask what it means that *Jesus* told this parable, and that the one who told *this* parable is the risen Lord of all, and that it was *Israel* who heard and believed or did not believe, and that it is the *church* that retells it. When the preacher has worked out what place Jesus' telling of this precise parable has in Jesus' story as the climax of Israel's story, and what precise place the church's retelling of the parable has in Jesus' story with the church, the preacher *has* his or her sermon.[26]

Two theological questions are uppermost for the preacher: What is God doing in or behind this text? and What doctrine or teaching of the church most closely connects to the biblical text? By answering, a preacher says, "The interpretation I am offering fits in this

153

place on the web of Christian narrative and meaning." In order to ensure sermon unity, preachers would do best to identify their doctrine by identifying that which comes closest to expressing the sermon's theme sentence or God sense. I need not say much more here except to encourage use of tables of contents and indexes in books of systematic theology as a way to locate the appropriate doctrines.[27] These teachings inform the sermon directly or indirectly as background material that deepens the preacher's thought. The preacher needs to decide what portion of a doctrine can be handled on a Sunday. Every page of the sermon needs theological movement, which is to say that on each page an idea grows that leads the hearer to deeper self-awareness or social consciousness before God and deeper understanding of God.

One further aspect of the cross and resurrection at the heart of our faith that deserves attention here is what I call a resurrection hermeneutic. The resurrection is a lens with which to interpret a biblical text. The resurrection can be read back into the words of Jesus, particularly to words that have a future component, to discern how the resurrection affects them. Said another way, individual texts point to the outcome, and the outcome points to individual texts. They are one story, one canonical fabric; thus the meaning of either cannot appropriately be conceived entirely separate from the other.

Matthew 25:31-46, the sheep and goats, portrays "The Judgment of the Nations." The multitudes are divided as sheep from goats according to their rewards of eternal punishment or eternal life. Evil does not win out, and there are consequences for sinful acts. Perhaps there are times when this can be and needs to be the fullness of the sermon's message, but this nonetheless falls short of the fullness of the gospel. If truth be told we are all goats, and not one of us is without sin. We can also hold out, alongside that judgment, for the One who comes to us from the cross and who died even for the goats (that is, the unrighteous). This angle does not erase the text but holds the cross in tension with it.

Matthew 22:15-22 includes the words, "Give therefore to the emperor the things that are the emperor's, and to God the things that are God's." When we use the cross and resurrection to read this text, we recognize that none of us is worthy, and none of us is capable of giving as Jesus asks. Only Christ is capable of giving to

God the things that are God's (that is, one's whole self and entire life). The early church is close to this understanding when it read this text in light of the *imago Dei*—we are stamped in the image of our Creator. Only by God's grace, by participating in Christ's death and resurrection through our baptism, is fulfilling this commandment made possible. Also, we can say of Matthew 23:1-12 (especially v. 12, "All who exalt themselves will be humbled, and all who humble themselves will be exalted") that in our baptism we are humbled, even to the point of dying to our old self; and we are exalted, given the name of Christ.

Every Bible text already exists in a complex framework of relationships with other texts or a web of Christian understanding. Making allegorical links in this manner is not innovative so much as it is descriptive of what already exists. It has to do with the analogy of faith guiding all biblical exegesis. Our ancestors understood better than we do that interpretation is to be consistent and congruent with the sum of faith and lead to reliance upon Jesus Christ.

Allegory as Prophecy (Anagogy)

We turn now to the third spiritual sense of scripture, anagogy, which deals with prophecy, eschatology, and the end times (or what we commonly associate with sermons that preach hellfire and brimstone). Anagogy is a dimension of allegory, for the early church arrived at anagogy by using the literal sense (when it dealt with these matters) or allegory. Allegory provides doctrinal understanding, and anagogy provides understandings of one particular doctrine. Anagogy is the prophetic sense, or mystical sense, that has to do with what happens when we die, the ascent of the soul to union with Christ, the Second Coming of Christ, and millennialism. The root meaning of anagogy is "to lead up" as is plain from this reflection on the four senses by Guibert DeNogent around 1100, " . . . and the last is ascetics, or spiritual enlightenment, through which we who are about to treat of lofty and heavenly topics are led to a higher way of life."[28] Since the New Testament points to the future that its events anticipate, anagogy captures what our ancestors understood to be the true meaning of Scripture: "For only the anagogical sense can be the ultimate literal sense of the historical process itself, since God Himself is the *res ultima* toward which everything is intended and ordered."[29]

Anagogy is not handled much in pulpits today except at funerals and some Sundays in Advent and Lent when texts dealing with these matters are discussed. Perhaps preachers avoid eschatology because it is tough or because it has been misused to distort Scripture and to frighten people into the church (for example, by Hal Lindsay in *The Late Great Planet Earth* [Grand Rapids, Mich.: Zondervan, 1970]) or simply because preachers are not sure what to say. This is unfortunate, for eschatology is a doctrine of hope and promise. David Buttrick is concerned that as preachers "we should be able to identify God's activity in the world" and "a sense of the presence of God-with-us seems to have vanished." The solution is to preach God's future, to picture in sermons the new age with vivid images of God's intent for the world: "Eschatology is not merely future hope but is the presence of the future among us."[30]

The doctrine of creation is at the beginning of the Christian story, and eschatology is at the end. Preachers need to be as comfortable dealing with one as the other. Why would we even bother preaching if the end of the story is other than God wins? As Barth laments, we end up in the situation of "adding at the conclusion of Christian Dogmatics a short and perfectly harmless chapter entitled— 'Eschatology.'"[31] Eschatology is anything but harmless.

The end of the story affects how we read every chapter of Scripture and life; any biblical text provides an opportunity to refer to the end of the story. The prophetic sense requires careful balancing, for the kingdom or realm of God is "here now" and "not yet"; is something humans work toward and something God ushers in; is both the fulfillment of human history and the purpose of all creation; involves both personal and corporate salvation; and occurs both in time and out of time. Several dimensions of eschatology need particular pulpit attention:

- The Second Coming of Christ is the fulfillment of all of God's purposes for creation including personal life.
- The Second Coming of Christ is a time of judgment of the world in which evil will finally be overcome.
- The resurrection of the body is something in which we now participate through baptism.
- The resurrection of the body that occurs in the parousia is the restoration of all relationships in union with Christ.

- Heaven is something we have already tasted in the love of God in Christ through the power of the Holy Spirit.
- Heaven is the eternal knowledge and experience of God's justice, mercy, peace, and love in contrast to the warning of hell and final destruction.

Reinhold Niebuhr warns against Christians claiming "any knowledge of either the furniture of heaven or the temperature of hell."[32] Most theologians recognize that biblical language about the future is highly metaphoric and needs to be treated as such. Shirley Guthrie has helpful suggestions for preachers. He encourages preachers to speak: not literally of how things will be but of the fact that God is at the end of history as Judge and Savior; not literally of where and how we will exist at the conclusion of time but of who we will be and what it means to be separated from or with God; not of one unified picture of the end times but of the many pictures Scripture offers; and using what we know God has done in the past as the best means of speaking about how God will act in the future.[33]

Here is a sampling of how preachers have handled such issues using the symbolic language of the Bible in imaginative ways. Most of the examples are from former times when anagogy was not yet largely abandoned and had a regular presence in sermons. Its use need not be lengthy, for often just a passing reference can help put life in perspective, as in this comment attributed to Luther: "If I knew that tomorrow the world would be destroyed, I would still plant an apple tree today."[34] Charles Spurgeon (1835–1892), preaching on 1 Corinthians 15:55 ("Where, O death, is your sting"), says that for many people death is not "the monster" they thought it to be, "it is the shutting of the eye on earth and the opening of it in heaven."[35] I. S. Spencer, referring to the same text from his Brooklyn pulpit in the late 1800s, observes, "Oh death, where is thy sting? Death may be a terror to nature; but death is the servant of the Christian. Death is yours. Ye are not death's. He shall not hurt you. All he can do is to take up the trembling believer, and put him into the arms of Jesus Christ."[36]

John Donne (1572–1631) writes in an age of much death and sees the death of six of his own children and of his wife, and he speaks with poignancy:

> . . . but if we be content so to depart into the wombe of the Earth, our grave, as that we know that, to be but the Entry into glory, as

we depart contentedly, so we shall rise gloriously, to that place, where our eternal Rest shall be, though here there be not our Rest; for he that shoots an arrow at a mark, yet means to put that arrow into his quiver again; and God that glorifies himselfe, in laying down our bodies in the grave, means also to glorifie them, in reassuming them to himselfe, at the last day.[37]

Joseph's prophecy on his deathbed in Genesis 50:24-26 provides Frederick W. Robertson an opportunity to speak of Joseph's authentic faith and to meditate on death in general:

When the coffin is lowered into the grave, and the dull, heavy sound of earth falling on it is heard, there are some to whom that sound seems but an echo of their worst anticipations; seems but to reverberate the idea of decay for ever, in the words, "Earth to earth, ashes to ashes, dust to dust." There are others, to whom it sounds pregnant with the expectations of immortality, the "sure and certain hope of a resurrection to eternal life." The difference between these two feelings is measured by the difference of lives. They whose life is low and earthly, how can they believe in aught beyond the grave, when nothing of that life which is eternal has yet stirred within them? They who have lived as Joseph lived, just in proportion to their purity and their unselfishness, must believe it. They cannot but believe it. The eternal existence is already pulsing in their veins. . . .

For what is our proof of immortality? Not the analogies of nature. . . . Not even the testimony to the fact of risen dead. . . . No, the life of the Spirit is the evidence. Heaven begun is the living proof that makes the heaven to come credible. . . . He alone can believe in immortality, who feels the resurrection in him.[38]

Arthur John Gossip in the 1920s preached with reference to the occasion of his wife's death:

Or, seeing that [death] has to be, will we not give [our dearest] willingly and proudly, looking God in the eyes, and telling Him that we prefer our loneliness rather than that they should miss one tittle of their rights. . . .

When we are young, heaven is a vague and nebulous and shadowy place. But as our friends gather there, more and more it gains body and vividness and homeliness. And when our dearest have passed yonder, how real and evident it grows, how near it is, how often we steal yonder. For, as the Master put it: Where our treasure is, there will our heart be also. Never again will I give out that stupid lie, "There is a happy land, far, far away." It is not far. They are quite near. And the communion of the saints is a tremendous and most blessed fact.

Nowadays, for example, to pray is to turn home. For then they run to meet us, draw us with their dear familiar hands into the Presence, stand quite close to us the whole time we are there—quite close, while we are there.[39]

While our own age can learn from how our preaching forebears spoke of death and the final things, we as preachers have much work to do to broaden their discussions to include issues of justice, equality, peace, and the environment in terms of the final picture. Perhaps the most famous of this consummation of "all things" is Martin Luther King, Jr.'s "I Have a Dream" sermon, which speaks at once of the victory of the Civil Rights movement and the vision of how things are intended to be in God's eternal realm.[40] Prophetic references of this sort need not be long, as in Elizabeth Achtemeier's sermon that discusses in part the tragic state of many cities:

And so we know in Jesus Christ that Zechariah's promise will finally be fully fulfilled, and that our city, and the cities of the world, will become faithful cities. God will dwell in the midst of us, as our Ruler and Father. And old men and old women shall again sit in the park, each with staff in hand for very age. And the streets of our city shall be full of boys and girls, playing in the squares.[41]

One final example should serve us well. Cornelius Plantinga, Jr., preaches thus:

Jesus' words are meant to raise our heads and raise our hopes. Could justice really come to the earth? Could husbands quit beating up their wives, and could wives quit blaming themselves? Could Yasir Arafat [leader of the Palestine Liberation Organization] and Ehud Barak [Prime Minister of Israel] look into each other's eyes and see a brother? Could some of us who struggle with addictions or with diseases that trap us—could we be liberated by God and start to walk tall in the kingdom of God? Could Jesus Christ appear among us in some way that our poverty-stricken minds can never imagine in a scenario that would simply erase our smug confidence about where the lines of reality are drawn?

If we believe in the kingdom of God we will pray, and we will hope for those without much hope left.[42]

We can at least dream dreams in our sermons, using clues from biblical texts, about how the tough issues of our times will be resolved in God's time. Moreover, we can not only speak of a futurist eschatology but also allow some dimension of a realized eschatology recognizing that Jesus' coming inaugurates the Realm of God on Earth. We already taste the future in the present.

Conclusion

Anagogy is the right place to end our journey through the four senses of Scripture. We have used the senses as instruments to identify some of the many lenses that preachers use today in reading the Bible. Each of the senses provides us with many ways of looking at Scripture, and more lenses cannot be our subject here: We are not able to explore literary criticism here as deeply as it deserves or even to begin to discuss lenses of race, gender, economic strata, and the like. What we have been able to do is focus on the theological lenses and God sense our ancestors knew so well and that we need so desperately to recover.

Our ancestors have left us a rich heritage in their four senses. Plainly, as preachers we cannot naïvely adopt the fourfold exegetical method any more than we could naïvely accept that the literal sense supplied by historical and literary criticism on its own is adequate for preaching. Rather, we need to adapt the best practices of our ancestors to meet the church's needs today. They knew that the purpose of preaching was to communicate a lively sense of God and a God-centered understanding of Scripture. For most of church history, this God sense is the literal sense of Scripture and while our forebears lacked the critical tools to root that understanding in history, Augustine and others at least anticipated the need in their adoption of a double-literal sense. We also need a double-literal sense to affirm that we are not ready to preach until we have married the historical- and literary-critical sense with the theological-critical sense.

It is now time that we put to rest any lingering wish that historical or literary critical exegesis leads directly to the pulpit. It certainly leads to what the text actually or literally says. It also leads to the best historical understanding we can have of what the text meant for its original human authors and their communities, and it may lead to theological insight as well. It does this by the only means that can guarantee some measure of stability in the biblical text, without which Scripture ceases to function as the norm for faith and life. We bring to our exegetical studies historical methods, documents, and understandings from the social sciences. Exegesis leads out, yet the founders of deconstruction show that we find in a text something of what we bring to it. Although we might yearn for a standard more "scientific" or "absolute," we necessarily recognize the limitation of any approach we take, and thereby also we remain open to other ways of reading Scripture, even those which do not seem to hold much promise for preaching, per se.

A single sense of Scripture is no longer possible. Theological criticism allows faith to "lead out" from the text what we discover about God in or behind it. The historical and theological processes are similar, but the knowledge upon which each draws is different; and they need to be deliberate, otherwise preachers will overlook one or the other. Both contribute to the God sense. Both need to flow if the Bible is to function as Scripture and the church is to have renewed confidence in preaching. Still, preachers are not accustomed to think of theological criticism as exegesis.

A similar process of exegesis is described by homiletical criticism that descends from the spiritual senses of our ancestors. Homiletical criticism is like literary criticism, commonly functioning on a synchronic axis with the text, discerning meaning in the present moment within and in front of the text. In reading a biblical text for moral purpose, a preacher connects what God is doing in a biblical text with what the congregation may be called to do, though a connection cannot be a law unmitigated by the gospel. Rather, it is an invitation to a more fulsome expression of faith through practice that, on one hand, comes as a demand, and on the other, as a promise fulfilled by Christ on the cross. We preach the one not to erase it with the other but to put them in tension with each other, for it is in this tension that the individual must work out her or his own salvation "with fear and trembling" (Phil. 2:12).

The same process of the text "leading out" continues through the entire homiletical endeavor, and thus the act of biblical interpretation is over not prior to sermon composition but only when the sermon is finally delivered and no more changes are possible. Our ancient ancestors caged bad allegory, which still occasionally escapes, but the good allegory they pioneered continues with refinement as a paradigm for how interpretation works. Because the biblical text is not in the sermon, only an image of it, the interpretation stands alongside it. The paradigm of allegory says "this grid of meanings in the sermon is that grid of meanings in the text," and allows for multiple points of dialogue between them. When preachers link a biblical text with some other biblical text or some specific situation in our world, they establish connections between different grids. Awareness of good allegory helps to avoid bad allegory.

We conceive of biblical interpretation for preaching as the union of all three kinds of criticism, although with regard to homiletical criticism and sermon form we mostly leave to other books how best actually to structure the sermon. Preachers are not used to thinking in terms of a trinity of critical approaches. Failure to recognize this trinity within homiletics allows some people in other disciplines to assess homiletics at superficial levels and allows some people within homiletics mistakenly to reject entirely any association with "method," critical or otherwise.

It is my understanding that conceiving of homiletics in this trinitarian manner describes what preachers actually do with Scripture. By setting out these criticisms as different tasks, preachers can have a fuller view of their work and be freed to read Scripture with new lenses including those pioneered and refined by our forebears. This project serves as an invitation to be more faith-centered in reading Scripture and more creative in finding ways to communicate Scripture authentically in sermons.

Along the journey to this spot, we have occasionally had glimpses of a certain poetry in the ancient way of reading Scripture viewed as a whole. Some Christians in a postmodern age might look back with a hint of envy to the unity of the ancient worldview in which Scripture, science, and theology all are interwoven parts of the same divine cloth and the world fits into a neat plan as surely as Scripture is composed by a loving God speaking in and through every part of it to the current age. This is a world in which all things point to Christ, and everything moves in grand symphony to further God's purpose. Of course, we may equally look at that same worldview rather cynically because we see that, historically, it can lead to resistance to science and history or, socially, to intolerance, bigotry, and oppression of those who do not share our perspectives. Our purpose here is not to rediscover the poetry of the ancient worldview so much as it is to recover a mature, faith-centered approach to Scripture for preaching today. For all of the oceans of change that have washed over our shores between "then" and "now," still there is a poetry to our own Christian understanding. If the music of our expression is more confined to our own time and culture and if we can no longer expect to be heard universally in the same way, the song we sing nonetheless still carries many of the same types, themes, and harmonies that our ancestors sang, and it allows us to recognize the importance of our own voices in the choirs of all times that continue to sing hymns of God's praise.

Summary Questions for Further Homiletical (Allegorical and Prophetic) Exegesis

1. Have I established meaningful connections between the text and now?
2. What concerns of the text can I identify?
3. What concerns of the sermon derive from these?
4. Have I expressed these concerns as short sentences (that is, no compound clauses)?
5. Are they complete sentences?
6. Have I chosen only the best for development (that is, a total of two or three pairs)?
7. Does my major concern of the text (that is, the main theme or the God sense) focus on God's action of grace?
8. Does the concern of the text chosen for "page one" anticipate the major concern?
9. In transposing (to concerns of the sermon) have I changed only one term?
10. Have I used critical theological thought in choosing my transpositions (that is, do they say something meaningful in themselves)?
11. Have I established meaningful connections between the text and other biblical texts?
12. Have I ensured that these connections are obvious and immediate?
13. Have I quoted other relevant scriptural verses to add depth and texture?

14. Have I considered using other biblical stories as examples of what this text discusses?
15. Have I made a link with one of the macrostories in the Bible (for example, Christus Victor/exodus; Christ as sacrifice/priestly sacrifice; and Christ as revealer/ saved from exile)?
16. Have I established meaningful connections between the text and the church's teachings?
17. What doctrine best expresses the major concern of the text?
18. What aspects of that doctrine can be developed in this sermon?
19. Do my concerns of the sermon invite theological development?
20. Does each page of the sermon demonstrate theological movement?
21. What difference does it make if Jesus speaks this text? That the speaker is the risen Lord of all?
22. What difference does it make that the speaker of another text is a true prophet?
23. What difference does it make that Israel hears and believes this text (or does not believe)? Or that the church retells it?
24. Can a resurrection hermeneutic be used with this text (i.e., is the import of Jesus' own words affected by his resurrection)?
25. Have I used the prophetic sense to point from the text to the end times?
26. Does the end of all things infuse my text and the present with hope?
27. Have I focused less on how it will be and more on the nature of God who reigns eternal?
28. Have I dreamt of justice, equality, peace, and restored creation in the final picture?
29. Have I allowed for expressions of realized eschatology (that is, the future present)?
30. Have I avoided describing the "furniture of heaven" and "the temperature of hell"?

God's Medicine

(A Sermon on Luke 3:1-18,
preached December 10, 2000)

When I was five, living in the north side of Edmonton, each day after breakfast our mother would make me and my sisters take our medicine from two brown glass bottles. In the bottle with the white top were the big fat red vitamin pills. The trick with the vitamin pill was to get it in your mouth, get both hands on a glass, and get it to your mouth to swallow before you were sidetracked into conversation and the pill began to dissolve in your mouth. That taste was bad enough. In the second bottle was something even worse—cod liver oil. There was no escaping the foul taste and feel of the cod liver oil, a teaspoonful, for this was before it came in capsules. Even knowing it would make you strong and healthy did not help. Sometimes even knowing what is good for us does not help us do what is right; that is the way for many of us with salvation. We know what we need to do, but we do not do it.

In the earliest surviving photographs of John the Baptist, he is standing in the wilderness preaching the coming of Jesus, while in the background between some boulders is a white tent marked with a big red cross. I suspect the photos are doctored. We do know for certain that John dispenses a nasty dose of bad-tasting medicine to everyone who comes out to see him. Everyone who makes the long trek from Jerusalem out to the desert by the Jordan River where he preaches, everyone has to swallow the medicine he doles out. To some he says, "You brood of vipers, who warned you to flee from the wrath to come?" To some he says, "Bear fruits worthy of repentance." To some he says, "Do not begin to say to yourselves, 'We have Abraham as our ancestor.' " To these same people he says, "See all of the rocks that litter the ground, as far as the eye can see? God can raise up children even from these stones. Don't show me your birth certificates and passports; I don't care where you were born; I don't care whose picture is in your family album; and I don't care whose portrait is above your mantel; and I do not care about your grandmother's maiden name. God is coming, so get ready to stand before your Maker. When you stand before God, there are no family passes or free tickets; and there is no cousin standing at a side door holding it open for you to slip in the back way. When you stand before God, your excellent inheritance is of no significance, and what fine family you marry is secondary. You stand before God alone, just you and your deeds, and you have to give an account of yourself and take responsibility. God is coming, and God is going to catch you out."

John the Baptist never took a night school course on How to Make Friends and Influence People. He does not care how many people are upset with him after church on the church steps. After he preaches he does not stand greeting people wishing them the best of the season or Merry Christmas. Why should you have a merry Christmas if you do not know your Savior? There is no reason to be happy. He calls it like he sees it. He specializes in making people feel bad because they have reason to feel bad. They need to repent, change their lives, make straight the way of the Lord. They are into comfortable grooves. For four hundred years there is no real prophet in Israel. They have not heard a good fire-and-brimstone sermon for a long time, and here is a real barn burner scorching the very hems of their garments. Some of those listening to John preach might rather risk the "wrath to come" than to experience it in the present coming from John. We know that John the Baptist makes people feel bad, feel like repenting. They want to know what they have to do to get right with God. And he tells them, each one, gives each of them a little dose of private medicine designed to taste bad.

But I do not need to tell you about John the Baptist. You all meet him, hear him, have him in your face with a spoonfull of medicine designed for you. Perhaps it was the other morning with the first snow, and like me, you were trying to decide which coat to wear. The light blue trench coat is only cotton but with a sports jacket it would do; or I could wear the other one that is more formal; or perhaps it is cold enough for the long winter coat with the belt, the one I have not worn for seven years; or here is the Eddie Bauer waterproof windbreaker—I did not even finish the count when

John the Baptist jumps out of the closet from behind all the coats and skowls, "Whoever has two coats must share with anyone who has none." To the person who is thinking of cheating on tax returns, John the Baptist this week comes hollering, "Keep no more for yourself than you are allowed." We are not being fair to John the Baptist if we equate him with guilt twinges we may have when our fingers close on an extra shortbread cookie or slice of Christmas cake. John is not concerned with trivial things. It is not an issue how many chocolates you have in your mouth or what color you are painting your living room. John is concerned with big things, with us preparing the way for the coming of the Lord. He wants to know what stands between you and God or you and your neighbor. What is wrong with your soul? What sin in your life is acting like Lake Ontario at the end of one of these side streets, preventing you from getting from here to the other side where eternal salvation awaits? John the Baptist has some nasty tasting medicine for each one of us because each of us has something that does not belong in one of God's saints. Sit down and open your mouth wide, and John will feed you that unpleasant medicine you have been avoiding. In comparison to what Dr. John the Baptist is going to give us, cod liver oil tastes good; we are going to wish we had some to rinse our mouths out after we taste what he has in store.

I could wish that John the Baptist really were around, not just his message. Our college community had a tragedy ten days ago. We had two students, a mother and a son, both active church people, and the son killed the mother in an act of mental illness. What good was John the Baptist's warning message? In the memorial service, we held both mother and son in prayer. This week was the twelfth anniversary of the killing of fourteen women engineering students at L'école Polytechnique in Montreal by a man who hates women. Where was John the Baptist with his warning message when that occurred? He was not there. He is, after all, just a prophet; if we want hope, we have to look to the One to whom he pointed, the Messiah, Jesus Christ.

In fact, we can straighten all we want and we still will not get life right before God. We can prepare for the Messiah's coming; we can start in the basement and work our way up to the attic, as we should; we can work from now until the twilight of our days, as we must; and still, still we will not get things right with God. No matter how long or hard we work, we are not going to accomplish our own salvation. When the sun is about to set we will still need God. All our preparation does not remove our need for a Savior. Help us, Lord. God knows that we mess up. Paul says, "The good that I would do I do not and the evil I would avoid I end up doing." God knows we cannot save ourselves. When we see John the Baptist out in the wilderness, we see God at work. God is taking charge. God is preparing the way for Christ. That is God's doing. God appoints John to be a prophet before he is born to Elizabeth and Zachariah; God calls John out to the wilderness to preach; God gives him a strong voice to reach all the crowds; God gives him conviction so he can proclaim; God gives him truth to preach; God gives him the gift of the Spirit so that he can commune with God and have faith and courage. From the beginning to the end of John's story, God is at work preparing the way for our Messiah.

God is at work, and John knows it. John is not happy when the members of the clergy, the religious authorities from Jerusalem, come out to meet him: "You brood of vipers," he says. "Who told you to flee from the wrath to come?" He personally wishes that they would not have a chance to change their ways and that they would meet the destruction they deserve. But even in asking "Who told you to flee from the wrath to come?" he knows the answer to his own question—God told them. God told them to flee the wrath to come. God is preparing the way for the coming of his Son, Jesus Christ. God has been trying to show people the way to eternal life since the beginning of time, and God knows that if it is going to happen, it will not be our doing. We are not going to save ourselves. God is going to have to do it for us.

And that is what this season is all about. God is readying us for our salvation, and readying our Salvation for us. Is there some valley of depression in your life that seems too hard for you to climb out of? Is there some mountain that is too high an obstacle to peace in your life for you to overcome? Are you feeling lost, without any straight sense of direction? The sweet words of the prophet Isaiah are coming true: "Every valley shall be filled, and every mountain and hill shall be made low, and the crooked shall be made straight, and the rough ways made smooth; and all flesh shall see the salvation of God" [Luke 3:5-6]. There is no problem too big, there is no sin that is too bad, there is no hurt that is so great that the coming One cannot take care of it.

I was down in Dallas a week ago where I heard a man speak of his high school years. He loved to play football; lived for it; was a star quarterback. But he developed back problems and had to give it up and wear a back brace. He developed nearsightedness so he had to start wearing horn-rim glasses. His girlfriend dumped him. He developed a bad case of acne. He found it hard to feel good about himself. Each morning his mother would come into his room while it was still dark to wake him for school. She would sit on the edge of his bed and gently—ever so gently—she would put her hand on his shoulder and use a rocking movement, back and forth, back and forth. All the while she would say in her southern drawl, "You so purdy. You so purdy."[1] This to a boy who can barely stand himself, told to him so that they are the first words he hears each day.

So it is with God in coming to us at this time. The hand of God is stretched out on the cradle of this Earth, and God says to humanity, "You so purdy. You so purdy." Prepare your hearts for your Savior. God's medicine is coming. You may be surprised how it tastes. Do not be surprised if it tastes and smells as sweet as the brow of a sleeping baby.

Notes

1. Reading Scripture with Many Lenses

1. Athanasius of Alexandria, for example, finds in the Psalms, meanings of texts from all over the Old Testament including the prophets: "the prophetic books are indicated in almost every psalm" and tell of a detailed awareness of the coming of Christ. See, Athanasius of Alexandria, "On the Interpretation of the Psalms," in Charles Kannengiesser, ed., *Early Christian Spirituality, Sources of Early Christian Thought* (Philadelphia: Fortress Press, 1986), p. 58.

2. Hugh of St. Victor, *The Didascalicon of Hugh of St. Victor: A Medieval Guide to the Arts*, trans. Jerome Taylor (New York and London: Columbia University Press, 1961), 2:4, p. 64.

3. Ibid., 6:5, p. 145.

4. For a brief list of gods and heroes in Homer and the allegorical equivalencies they were assigned by ancient interpreters see Karlfried Froehlich, ed., *Biblical Interpretation in the Early Church* (Philadelphia: Fortress Press, 1984), p. 19.

5. Philo, "The Contemplative Life," *Philo*, Loeb Classical Library, Vol. IX (London: William Heinemann/Cambridge, Mass.: Harvard University Press, 1954), pp. 78, 161.

6. Origen, *On First Principles*, trans. G. W. Butterworth (London: SPCK, 1936), IV, 2:4, p. 276.

7. To the literal (historical) and allegorical he adds the analogical (demonstrating the congruence of Old and New Testaments) and the etiological (giving the causes of things said and done). "On the Profit of Believing," trans. C. L. Cornish, in Philip Schaff, ed., *Nicene and Post-Nicene Fathers of the Christian Church, vol. III, St. Augustine: On the Holy Trinity, Doctrine and Treatises, Moral Treaties* (Edinburgh: T & T Clark/Grand Rapids, Mich.: William B. Eerdmans Publishing Company, 1993), p. 349.

8. James Samuel Preus, *From Shadow to Promise: Old Testament Interpretation from Augustine to the Young Luther* (Cambridge, Mass.: The Belknap Press of Harvard University Press, 1969), pp. 21-22.

9. Augustine of Dacia has "anagogy is what you hope for" as the second line of the distich (i.e., *Moralis quid agas, quid speres anagogia*). See "Augustini de Dacia O.P. 'Rotulus Pugillaris'" P. A. Walz, ed., in *Angelicum* (Rome: Pontifical Institute International, 1929), p. 256. The original source is often incorrectly cited as Nicholas of Lyra. Henri de Lubac, *Medieval Exegesis*, vol. 1, *The Four Senses of Scripture*, trans. Mark Sebanc (Grand Rapids, Mich.: William B. Eerdmans Publishing Company; Edinburgh, Scotland: T & T Clark, 1998), pp. 1-2. Originally published as *Exégèse médiévale: 1: Les Quatres Sens de L'ecriture* (Paris: Editions Montaigne, 1959).

10. Christopher Ocker, "Biblical Interpretation in the Middle Ages," in Donald K. McKim, ed., *Historical Handbook of Major Biblical Interpreters* (Downer's Grove, Ill. and Leicester, England: InterVarsity Press, 1998), pp. 80-81.

11. Robert Grant with David Tracy, *A Short History of the Interpretation of the Bible*, 2d ed. (Philadelphia: Fortress Press, 1984), p. 85. James Samuel Preus identifies the rhyme coming not directly from Bede but from the *Glosa ordinaria* from the school of Anselm of Laon: "history, which tells the *res gestae*; allegory, in which one thing is understood from another; tropology, i.e. moral pronouncement, which deals with the ordering of morals; anagogy, through which we are led to higher things in order to be drawn up to the highest and heavenly things." Preus, *From Shadow to Promise*, p. 26. See also Werner G. Jeanrond, *Theological Hermeneutics: Development and Significance* (New York: Crossroad, 1991), p. 27.

12. Cited by Jon Whitman, "Allegory," in T.V.F. Brogan, ed., *The New Princeton Handbook of Poetic Terms* (Princeton, N.J.: Princeton University Press, 1994), p. 9.

13. This unity of Scripture has been challenged, says Gerhard Ebeling, first, by the inability of Scripture to produce a unified theology of the two Testaments; second, by each Testament having an inner unity, and third, by the fact that outside historical sources are pertinent to the reading of the Bible. See Brevard S. Childs, *Biblical Theology of the Old and New Testaments: Theological Reflection on the Christian Bible* (Minneapolis: Fortress Press, 1993), p. 7.

14. G. R. Evans, *The Language and Logic of the Bible: The Earlier Middle Ages* (Cambridge, UK: Cambridge University Press, 1984), p. 1.

15. Two academic works of contrasting length were of particular help in signaling that a change in attitude was overdue in preaching. The first was de Lubac, *Exégèse médiévale*. The second was David C. Steinmetz, "The Superiority of Pre-Critical Exegesis," *Theology Today*, 37:1 (April, 1980): pp. 27-38. He seemed bold in identifying fourfold exegesis as "superior" to historical-critical approaches.

2. The Literal Sense and Historical-Critical Exegesis

1. Stephen Farris, *Preaching That Matters: The Bible and Our Lives* (Louisville: Westminster John Knox Press, 1998), p. 7.

2. "The Second Helvetic Confession," *The Book of Confessions, The Constitution of the Presbyterian Church (U.S.A.), Part I* (Louisville: The Office of the General Assembly, 1996), 5.010, p. 57.

3. "The Westminster Confession of Faith," in *The Book of Confessions*, I.7, 6.008, p. 127.

4. Gerhard von Rad, *Biblical Interpretations in Preaching*, trans. John E. Steely (Nashville: Abingdon Press, 1977 [1973]), p. 14.

5. Introduction to *The Holy Bible: New Living Translation* (Wheaton, Ill.: Tyndale House Publishers, 1996), p. xli.

6. "The Second Helvetic Confession," 5.004, p. 55.

7. "The Westminster Confession of Faith," I:8, 6.008, p. 127.

8. Hans Frei, *The Eclipse of Biblical Narrative* (New Haven, Conn.: Yale University Press, 1974).

9. Erich Auerbach, *Mimesis: The Representation of Reality in Western Literature,*

trans. Willard R. Trask (Princeton, N.J.: Princeton University Press, 1953; reprint Doubleday, 1957).

10. Jacques Derrida, *Of Grammatology*, trans. Gayatri Chakravorty Spivak (Baltimore: The Johns Hopkins University Press, 1976 [1967]), pp. 65, 71.

11. Paul Tillich, *Dynamics of Faith* (New York: Harper & Row, 1957), pp. 52-53.

12. On this controversy, see for instance, Luke Timothy Johnson, *The Real Jesus: The Misguided Quest for the Historical Jesus and the Truth of the Traditional Gospels* (San Francisco: Harper San Francisco, 1996).

13. I am grateful in this section to Albert M. Sanford, *Literalistic Interpretations of the Scriptures, The Ryerson Essays, Number 8* (Toronto: The Ryerson Press, 1922), pp. 7-24.

14. Sandra M. Schneiders, *The Revelatory Text: Interpreting the New Testament as Sacred Scripture* (New York: HarperSanFrancisco, 1991), p. 162.

15. Students wanting a fuller treatment of these matters may consult Farris, *Preaching That Matters*, 39-124, or Paul Scott Wilson, *The Practice of Preaching* (Nashville: Abingdon Press, 1995), esp. pp. 128-76.

16. Carl E. Braaten and Robert W. Jenson, eds., *Reclaiming the Bible for The Church* (Grand Rapids, Mich. and Cambridge, UK: William B. Eerdmans Publishing Company, 1995).

17. Stephen E. Fowl, ed., *The Theological Interpretation of Scripture: Classic and Contemporary Readings* (Cambridge, Mass. and Oxford, UK: Blackwell Publishers, 1997).

18. See Paul Scott Wilson, *The Four Pages of the Sermon: A Guide to Biblical Preaching* (Nashville: Abingdon Press, 1999), pp. 159-161.

19. Ibid., esp. pp. 82-89. Movie making is no guarantee against bad historical information, however.

3. A Brief History of the Literal Sense

1. James Samuel Preus, *From Shadow to Promise: Old Testament Interpretation from Augustine to the Young Luther* (Cambridge, Mass.: The Belknap Press of Harvard University Press, 1969), 3. Only in Luther, he argues, is the integrity of the Old Testament history, word, and faith decisively recovered for the church.

2. Origen, *On First Principles*, trans. G. W. Butterworth (London: SPCK, 1936), IV, 2:6, p. 279.

3. Ibid., IV, 2:9, pp. 286-87.

4. Ibid., IV, 3:1, pp. 288-89.

5. Ibid., IV, 3:3, p. 292.

6. Beryl Smalley, *The Study of the Bible in the Middle Ages* (Oxford, UK: The Clarendon Press, 1941), p. 11.

7. Augustine, *On Christian Doctrine*, trans. D. W. Robertson, Jr. (Indianapolis/New York: Bobbs-Merrill Co., 1958). All citations are from this edition.

8. Godfrey of St. Victor, "Fons philosophia," Henri de Lubac, *Medieval Exegesis*, vol. 1, *The Four Senses of Scripture*, trans. Mark Sebanc (Grand Rapids, Mich.: William B. Eerdmans Publishing Company; Edinburgh, Scotland: T & T Clark, 1998), p. 3.

9. Augustine, *The City of God*, vol. 2 of *A Select Library of the Post-Nicene Fathers of the Christian Church*, Philip Schaff, ed. (Edinburgh, Scotland: T & T Clark; Grand Rapids, Mich.: William B. Eerdmans Publishing Company, 1993), p. 308.

10. Augustine, "The Harmony of the Gospels," in vol. 6 of Schaff, *Nicene and Post-Nicene Fathers*, p. 120.

11. Ibid.

12. Ibid., p. 146.

13. Ibid., p. 149.

14. Augustine, "The Ten Virgins," in *Great Sermons of the World*, Clarence E. Macartney, ed. (Peabody, Mass.: Hendrickson Publishers, 1997), p. 47.

15. Ibid., p. 51.

16. Augustine, *City of God*, p. 307.

17. Preus, *From Shadow to Promise*, p. 14.

18. Origen says, "The splendour of Christ's advent has, therefore, by illuminating the law of Moses with the brightness of the truth, withdrawn the veil which had covered the letter of the law and has disclosed, for every one who believes in him, all those 'good things' which lay concealed within." *First Principles*, IV, 1:6, p. 265.

19. Hugh of St. Victor, *Patrologia Latina* 6, 3:799-802. Cited by Smalley, *Study of the Bible*, p. 62.

20. Hugh of St. Victor, *The Didascalicon of Hugh of St. Victor: A Medieval Guide to the Arts,* trans. Jerome Taylor (New York and London: Columbia University Press, 1961), 6:4, p. 144. "Exposition includes three things: the letter, the sense, and the deeper meaning *(sententia)*.... [E]very discourse ought to contain at least two. That discourse in which something is so clearly signified by the mere telling that nothing else is left to be supplied for its understanding contains only letter and sense. But that discourse in which the hearer can conceive nothing from the mere telling unless an exposition is added thereto contains only the letter and a deeper meaning." 6:8, p. 147. In this he anticipates a later distinction between what a text says and what it means.

21. Preus, *From Shadow to Promise*, p. 69.

22. Thomas Aquinas, *Summa Theologia,* Vol. 1, Thomas Gilby, ed. (London: Eyre & Spottiswoode; New York: McGraw-Hill, 1963), 1a.1, 10, pp. 37, 39.

23. Ibid., 1a.1, 10, p. 39.

24. Nicholas of Lyra, *Prologus secundus de intentione auctoris et modo*, cited by Preus, *From Shadow to Promise*, p. 68.

25. Corrine L. Patton, "Nicholas of Lyra (ca. 1270–1349)," Donald K. McKim, ed., *Historical Handbook of Major Biblical Interpreters* (Downer's Grove, Ill. and Leicester, England: InterVarsity Press, 1998), p. 117.

26. Martin Luther, "Answer to the Superchristian, Superspiritual, and Super-learned Book of Goat Emser of Leipzig," vol. 3 of *Works of Martin Luther* (Philadelphia: Muhlenberg Press, 1930), p. 349.

27. Ibid., p. 350.

28. Ibid.

29. "[In the Scriptures] you will find the swaddling cloths and the manger in which Christ lies." Martin Luther, "Preface to the Old Testament," vol. 35 of *Luther's Works,* ed. E. Theodore Bachmann (Philadelphia: Muhlenberg Press, 1960), p. 236.

30. William Adams Brown, *Modern Theology and the Preaching of the Gospel* (New York: Charles Scribner's Sons, 1914), p. 78.

31. On this point see Karlfried Froehlich "'Always to Keep the Literal Sense in Holy Scripture Means to Kill One's Soul': The State of Biblical Hermeneutics at the Beginning of the Fifteenth Century" in *Literary Uses of Typology from the Late Middle Ages to the Present*, Earl Miner, ed. (Princeton, N.J.: Princeton University Press, 1977), p. 20. Other reformers, like Matthias Flacius Illyricus, have a similar position: "Scripture has one goal; its entire message points above all, in its essence, to the Lamb of God, who takes away the sin of the world." Robert Kolb, "Flacius Illyricus, Matthias (1520–1575)," McKim, *Historical Handbook*, p. 192.

32. John Calvin, *Institutes of the Christian Religion*, John T. McNeil, ed. and trans. Ford Lewis Battles, vol. 20 of *The Library of Christian Classics* (Philadelphia: The Westminster Press, 1960), I, VII, p. 78.

33. Ibid., p. 80.

34. Elsie Anne McKee, "On Relating Calvin's Exegesis and Theology," in *Biblical Hermeneutics in Historical Perspective: Studies in Honor of Karlfried Froehlich on His Sixtieth Birthday*, Mark S. Burrows and Paul Rorem, eds. (Grand Rapids, Mich.: William B. Eerdmans Publishing Company, 1991), p. 221.

35. Ibid, p. 225.

36. Augustine, "Discourse on Psalm 3" in *St. Augustine on the Psalms*, trans. Dame Scholastica Hebgin and Dame Felicitas Corrigan, vol. 1 of *Ancient Christian Writers* (Westminster, Md.: The Newman Press, 1960), pp. 30-33.

37. John Calvin, *Commentary on the Book of Psalms*, vol. 1, trans. James Anderson (Grand Rapids, Mich.: Wm. B. Eerdmans Publishing Company, 1948), p. 33. See pp. 30-33.

38. Mark 10:3-4 was also used: " 'What did Moses Command you?' They said, 'Moses allowed a man to write a certificate of divorce.' " See John Rogerson, "Part I. The Old Testament" in Paul Avis, ed., John Rogerson, Christopher Rowland, and Barnabas Lindars, *The Study and Use of the Bible*, vol. 2 of *The History of Christian Theology* (Grand Rapids, Mich.: William B. Eerdmans Publishing Company; Basingstoke: Marshall Pickering, 1988), p. 97.

39. Carl E. Braaten and Robert W. Jenson, et al., eds., *Christian Dogmatics*, vol. 1 (Philadelphia: Fortress Press, 1984), p. xix.

40. John Q. Schneider, "Melanchthon, Philipp (1497–1560)," McKim, *Historical Handbook*, p. 227.

41. Matthias Flacius Illyricus, *Clavis Scriptura Sacra* (Basel: Jo. Operinum & Euseb. Episcopium, 1567). See Werner Georg Kümmel, *The New Testament: The History of the Investigation of Its Problems*, trans. S. McLean Gilmour and Howard C. Kee (Nashville and New York: Abingdon Press, 1972), p. 28.

42. Robert Kolb, "Flacius Illyricus, Matthias," in McKim, *Historical Handbook*, p. 193.

43. Cited by Gerald T. Sheppard, *The Future of the Bible: Beyond Liberalism and Literalism* (Toronto: The United Church Publishing House, 1990), p. 12.

44. Richard A. Muller, "Biblical Interpretation in the 16th & 17th Centuries," McKim, *Historical Handbook*, pp. 127-28.

45. See Gerald T. Sheppard, "Isaiah," *The HarperCollins Bible Commentary*,

James L. Mays, gen. ed. (San Francisco: HarperSanFrancisco, 2000), pp. 489-537.

46. See also David L. Bartlett's treatments of literary criticism for the Bible in his *Between the Bible and the Church: New Methods for Biblical Preaching* (Nashville: Abingdon Press, 1999), pp. 37-72; and A. K. Adams, ed., *Handbook of Postmodern Biblical Interpretation* (St. Louis: Chalice Press, 2000).

47. Brevard S. Childs, *Biblical Theology of the Old and New Testaments: Theological Reflection on the Christian Bible* (Minneapolis: Fortress Press, 1993), p. 99.

48. See Gerald T. Sheppard, "Childs, Brevard," McKim, *Historical Handbook*, pp. 575-84.

49. Childs, *Biblical Theology*, pp. 101-2.

50. Bartlett, *Between the Bible and the Church*, p. 65.

51. Raymond Brown, *The "Sensus Plenior" of Sacred Scripture* (Baltimore: St. Mary's University Press, 1955).

52. See, for example, Gail R. O'Day, *The Word Disclosed: John's Story and Narrative Preaching* (Philadelphia: Fortress Press, 1987).

53. Richard B. Hays, *The Moral Vision of the New Testament: A Contemporary Introduction to New Testament Ethics* (New York: HarperSanFrancisco, 1996). See especially part 2, "The Synthetic Task: Finding Coherence in the Moral Vision of the New Testament."

54. Walter Brueggemann, *Theology of the Old Testament: Testimony, Dispute, Advocacy* (Minneapolis: Fortress Press, 1997), pp. 118-19.

55. Ibid., p. 728.

56. Carl E. Braaten and Robert W. Jenson, eds., *Reclaiming the Bible for the Church* (Grand Rapids, Mich. and Cambridge, UK: William B. Eerdmans Publishing Company, 1995), p. x.

57. Childs, *Biblical Theology*, p. 9.

4. The Literal Sense and God

1. David E. Demson, *Hans Frei & Karl Barth: Different Ways of Reading Scripture* (Grand Rapids, Mich. and Cambridge, UK: William B. Eerdmans Publishing Company, 1997), p. 109.

2. Brevard S. Childs, *Biblical Theology of the Old and New Testaments: Theological Reflection on the Christian Bible* (Minneapolis: Fortress Press, 1993), p. 7.

3. Daniel Patte, *Ethics of Biblical Interpretation: a Reevaluation* (Louisville: Westminster John Knox Press, 1995), p. 119.

4. J. Richard Middleton and Brian J. Walsh, *Truth Is Stranger than it Used to Be: Biblical Faith in a Postmodern Age* (Downers Grove, Ill.: Intervarsity Press, 1995), esp. chap. 8.

5. Barnabas Lindars, "Part III. The New Testament," in Paul Avis, ed., John Rogerson, Christopher Rowland, and Barnabas Lindars, *The Study and Use of the Bible*, vol. 2 of *The History of Christian Theology* (Grand Rapids, Mich.: William B. Eerdmans Publishing Company; Basingstoke: Marshall Pickering, 1988), p. 382.

6. "Is the perception of New Testament times, when the pre-scientific understanding of life was very different from ours, indispensable, or can we not rather

acknowledge that miracles were commonly reported about holy people, and what matters is the teaching which these traditions convey?" Ibid., p. 395.

7. Elisabeth Schüssler Fiorenza, "Contemporary Biblical Scholarship: Its Roots, Present Understandings, and Future Directions," in Francis A. Eigo, ed., *Modern Biblical Scholarship: Its Impact on Theology and Proclamation* (Villanova, Penn.: The Villanova University Press, 1984), p. 3.

8. Ibid., pp. 27-28.

9. James Wm. McClendon, Jr., *Ethics: Systematic Theology, Volume 1* (Nashville: Abingdon Press, 1986), pp. 31-32.

10. Sandra M. Schneiders, *The Revelatory Text: Interpreting the New Testament as Sacred Scripture* (New York: HarperSanFrancisco, 1991), p. 109.

11. David L. Bartlett, *Between the Bible and the Church: New Methods for Biblical Preaching* (Nashville: Abingdon Press, 1999), p. 13.

12. Elizabeth Achtemeier, "The Canon as the Voice of the Living God," in Carl E. Braaten and Robert W. Jenson, eds., *Reclaiming the Bible for The Church* (Grand Rapids, Mich. and Cambridge, UK: William B. Eerdmans Publishing Company, 1995), p. 120.

13. Lauren Winner, "A Return to Tradition? Gen X Revisited," *The Christian Century* (Nov. 8, 2000): pp. 1146-47.

14. Robert W. Jenson, "Hermeneutics and the Life of the Church," in Braaten, et al., *Reclaiming*, 99. Jenson is simply one of several theologians who are focusing on the "theological perspective" of Scripture that Werner G. Jeanrond defines as "the question of God" and that he clarifies as "the nature of God and . . . God's relationship with humankind." See Werner G. Jeanrond, "After Hermeneutics: The Relationship Between Theology and Biblical Studies," in Francis Watson, *The Open Text: New Directions for Biblical Studies?* (London: SCM Press, 1993), pp. 88, 95. Stephen E. Fowl responds,

> While it is not clear what "the question of God" is, it is clear that the Bible presents a variety of diverse claims and pictures of God. What sort of attention to these accounts really counts as theological interpretation? Does an interpretation that attends to the picture of God found in the Succession Narrative wholly in terms of the social and political forces that led to the production of that particular view of God count as theological? If so, then the vast majority of professional biblical scholarship has been theological for quite some time.

Stephen E. Fowl, *Engaging Scripture: A Model for Theological Interpretation* (Malden, Mass. and Oxford, UK: Blackwell Publishers, 1998), p. 29.

15. James M. Gustafson, "Ways of Using Scripture" in Wayne G. Boulton, Thomas D. Kennedy, and Allen Verhey, eds., *From Christ to the World: Introductory Readings in Christian Ethics* (Grand Rapids, Mich.: William B. Eerdmans Publishing Company, 1994), p. 21. Originally published as "The Place of Scripture in Christian Ethics: A Methodological Study," in James M. Gustafson, *Theology and Christian Ethics* (Philadelphia: United Church Press, 1974).

16. Ibid., p. 24.

17. Personal conversation with Sarah Smith at the University of Toronto, June 20, 2000.

18. Jeanrond, "After Hermeneutics," in Watson, *Open Text*, p. 97.

19. See Richard Lischer, *A Theology of Preaching: the Dynamics of the Gospel* (Nashville: Abingdon Press, 1981), p. 61; Paul Scott Wilson, *Imagination of the Heart: New Understandings in Preaching* (Nashville: Abingdon Press, 1988), pp. 131-32; Paul Scott Wilson, *The Practice of Preaching* (Nashville: Abingdon Press, 1995), pp. 150-55; Ronald J. Allen, *Preaching the Topical Sermon* (Louisville: Westminster/John Knox Press, 1992), p. 64; Stephen Farris, *Preaching That Matters: The Bible and Our Lives* (Louisville: Westminster John Knox Press, 1998), pp. 122-24; Cleophus J. LaRue, *The Heart of Black Preaching* (Louisville: Westminster John Knox Press, 2000).

5. Theological Exegesis and the Literal Sense

1. These are difficult terms in part because of their history, and Luther uses them to distinguish between Old and New Testaments, which is not the sense in which homiletics has used them of late. Karl P. Donfried says, "It should be noted that the discussion of 'law and gospel' is thoroughly confused and confusing . . . in many parts of Lutheranism. The time has come to give up these shibboleths, and to describe what is intended in a non-ghettoized language that is intelligible to a wider audience and one in dialogue with the biblical studies on the subject." Karl P. DonFried, "Alien Hermeneutics and the Misappropriation of Scripture," in Carl E. Braaten and Robert W. Jenson, eds., *Reclaiming the Bible for The Church* (Grand Rapids, Mich. and Cambridge, UK: William B. Eerdmans Publishing Company, 1995), p. 29.

2. Richard Lischer, *A Theology of Preaching: the Dynamics of the Gospel* (Nashville: Abingdon Press, 1981), p. 61.

3. Hans Frei, "The 'Literal Reading' of Biblical Narrative in the Christian Tradition: Does It Stretch or Will It Break?" in Frank McConnell, ed., *The Bible and the Narrative Tradition* (New York and Oxford, UK: Oxford University Press, 1986), pp. 62-63.

6. The Spiritual Senses: An Introduction

1. Hugh of St. Victor, *The Didascalicon of Hugh of St. Victor: A Medieval Guide to the Arts*, trans. Jerome Taylor (New York and London: Columbia University Press, 1961), 6:4, p. 140.

2. St. Gregory, "*Moralia; Praef. In Iob* (Library of the Fathers)," in P. Migne, *Patrologia Latina*, vol. lxxvi, p. 18 (i, 6-7). For the English Translation, I used *Morals on the Book of Job, vol. 1* (Oxford: John Henry Parker/London: J. G. F. and J. Rivington, 1844), i, pp. 6-7.

3. David C. Steinmetz, "The Superiority of Pre-Critical Exegesis," *Theology Today*, 37:1 (April, 1980): pp. 29-30.

4. Alphonsus Liguori used to preach *de terrore* on his evangelical missions that formed the backbone of his developing Redemptorist Order of Preachers in the eighteenth century and that provided a blueprint for Protestant revivals. See "Preaching" in *The Complete Works of Saint Alphonsus Liguori*, vol. 15, trans. Eugene Grimm (New York: Benziger Brothers, 1890).

5. Thomas Aquinas, *Summa Theologia*, vol. 1, Thomas Gilby, ed. (London: Eyre & Spottiswoode; New York: McGraw-Hill, 1963), 1a.1, 10, p. 39. Aquinas notes that Hugh of St. Victor has only three senses, the historical, the tropological, and the allegorical, pp. 39-40. One of Aquinas's editors argues that Aquinas, in fact, has four senses: the primary literal, the fuller sense inspired by the Holy Spirit, the typical that seeks types, and the accommodated sense referring to applications that are perceived in the biblical text, pp. 177-178.

6. Hugh of St. Victor, *Didascalicon*, 5:2, pp. 120-21.

7. Henri de Lubac, *Medieval Exegesis*, vol. 1, *The Four Senses of Scripture*, trans. Mark Sebanc (Grand Rapids, Mich.: William B. Eerdmans Publishing Company; Edinburgh, Scotland: T & T Clark, 1998), pp. 7, 24, 90-96, 100, 106, 107, 112.

8. Giles of Paris uses the word typology for allegory here. de Lubac, *Medieval Exegesis*, p. 3.

7. The Moral Sense

1. A. G. Hebert, *The Authority of the Old Testament* (London: Faber & Faber, 1947), p. 269.

2. Preus notes, "The medieval answer to the question, 'What is the Bible all about?' could be summed up in three words: *doctrina*, *lex*, and *promissio*. The Bible teaches us what is to [be] believed *(credenda)*, loved *(diligenda)*, and hoped *(speranda)*." James Samuel Preus, *From Shadow to Promise: Old Testament Interpretation from Augustine to the Young Luther* (Cambridge, Mass.: The Belknap Press of Harvard University Press, 1969), p. 189. See also Augustine, *On Christian Doctrine*, I, 35, 39-40, 44; III, 10, 15.

3. Augustine, *On Christian Doctrine*, trans. D. W. Robertson, Jr. (Indianapolis / New York: Bobbs-Merrill Co., 1958), 3, XV.

4. Amanda Berry Wylie, "The Exegesis of History in John Chrysostom's Homilies on Acts," in *Biblical Hermeneutics in Historical Perspective: Studies in Honor of Karlfried Froehlich on His Sixtieth Birthday*, Mark S. Burrows and Paul Rorem, eds. (Grand Rapids, Mich.: William B. Eerdmans Publishing Company, 1991), p. 66.

5. Ambrose of Milan, "Concerning Virgins," Kannengiesser, *Early Christian Spirituality*, p. 94.

6. Martin D. Yaffe, ed., "Interpretative Essay" in *Thomas Aquinas, The Literal Exposition on Job: A Scriptural Commentary Concerning Providence*, trans. Anthony Damico (Atlanta: Scholars Press, 1989), p. 9.

7. Thomas of Chobham's *Summa de Arte Praedicatoria* (Cambridge Mass.: Corpus Christi College, MS 455 fo. 1rb.), G. R. Evans, *The Language and Logic of the Bible: The Earlier Middle Ages* (Cambridge, UK: Cambridge University Press, 1984), pp. 114-15.

8. Hugh of St. Victor, *The Didascalicon of Hugh of St. Victor: A Medieval Guide to the Arts*, trans. Jerome Taylor (New York and London: Columbia University Press, 1961), 5:9, p. 132.

9. Martin Luther, "How Christians Should Regard Moses," in *Luther's Works*, vol. 35, ed. E. Theodore Bachmann and Helmut Lehmann, trans. E. Theodore

Bachmann (Philadelphia: Muhlenberg Press, 1960), p. 174. For a discussion of Luther's so called "tower experience" that led him to conclude there were two kinds of Scripture, one that applied to him and the other that did not, see Eric W. Gritsch in Burrows, et al., *Biblical Hermeneutics*, p. 196: "Scripture becomes the Word of God [for Luther] when it pertains and applies to the turmoil *(Anfechtung)* in the interpreter's life."

10. Preus, *From Shadow to Promise*, pp. 233-34.

11. Hayes and Holladay note that, "even Jewish exegesis devised a fourfold interpretation of texts: (a) *peshat* (the plain meaning), (b) *remez* (allusion or allegory), (c) *derash* (the homiletical), and (d) *sod* (the mystical or secret)." John H. Hayes and Carl R. Holladay, *Biblical Exegesis: A Beginners Handbook* (Atlanta: John Knox Press, 1982), p. 21. Brevard S. Childs identifies the origin of this division between literal and homiletical among the Babylonian Amoraim in his, "The *Sensus Literalis* of Scripture: An Ancient and Modern Problem," *Beitrage zur alttestamentlichen Theologie: Festschrift fur Walther Zimmerli zum 70* (Gottingen: Vandenhoeck und Ruprecht, 1977), p. 80.

12. Alan of Lille, *The Art of Preaching, Cistercian Fathers Series*, 23, trans. Gilian R. Evans (Kalamazoo, Mich.: Cistercian Publications, 1981), p. 15.

13. Augustine, "Discourse on Psalm 3," in *St. Augustine on the Psalms*, trans. Dame Scholastica Hebgin and Dame Felicitas Corrigan, vol. 1 of *Ancient Christian Writers* (Westminster, Md.: The Newman Press, 1960), pp. 1, 31-32.

14. Beryl Smalley and G. Lacombe, "The Lombard's Commentary on Isaias and Other Fragments," *The New Scholasticism*, v (April 1931): pp. 123-196. Cited in Beryl Smalley, *The Study of the Bible in the Middle Ages* (Oxford, UK: The Clarendon Press, 1941), p. 109.

15. Bernard McGinn, et al., eds., "Sermon 86," in *Meister Eckhart: Teacher and Preacher* (Mahwah, N.J.: Paulist Press, 1986), pp. 343-44.

16. John Calvin, *Commentary on the Book of Psalms*, vol. 1, trans. James Anderson (Grand Rapids, Mich.: Wm. B. Eerdmans Publishing Company, 1948), pp. 27-33.

17. John Calvin, "Pure Preaching of the Word," in *The Mystery of Godliness: and Other Selected Sermons* (Grand Rapids, Mich.: Wm. B. Eerdmans Publishing Company, 1950), pp. 59-60.

18. Martin Luther, "A Brief Instruction on What to Look for and Expect in the Gospels," in *Luther's Works*, vol. 35, p. 118.

19. Luther, "Preface to the Epistle to the Romans, 1522," vol. 6 of the *Works of Martin Luther* (Philadelphia: Muhlenberg Press, 1932), pp. 456-57.

20. "So we must cling to the pure Scripture alone which teaches nothing but Christ so that we may attain piety through him in faith, and then do all our works in freedom for the benefit of our neighbor." Martin Luther, "The Gospel for the Festival of the Epiphany, Matthew 2[:1-11]," *Luther's Works, Sermons II*, Hans J. Hillerbrand, ed. (Philadelphia: Fortress Press, 1974), p. 173.

21. Hayden White, *The Historical Imagination in Nineteenth-Century Europe* (Baltimore and London: The Johns Hopkins University Press, 1973), p. 27.

22. James M. Gustafson, "Ways of Using Scripture" in Wayne G. Boulton, Thomas D. Kennedy, and Allen Verhey, eds., *From Christ to the World: Introductory Readings in Christian Ethics* (Grand Rapids, Mich.: William B. Eerdmans Publishing

Company, 1994), p. 23; originally published as "The Place of Scriptures in Christian Ethics: A Methodological Study," in *Theology and Christian Ethics* (Philadelphia: United Church Press, 1974).

23. Ibid., pp. 21-23. For purposes of clarity I have given titles to his four criteria.

24. Ibid., p. 23.

25. Ibid., p. 24.

26. Daniel Patte, *Ethics of Biblical Interpretation: a Reevaluation* (Louisville: Westminster John Knox Press, 1995), p. 125. In contrast to Gustafson, Patte does what he can to avoid any mention of God, perhaps because he sees much God language in what he considers the prison camp of fundamentalists. Still, from a preaching perspective, his silence is peculiar, given that he claims to value the authority of Scripture, and as a consequence, his argument for androcritical multidimensional exegesis seems to be alert to pluralism and blind to its own anthropocentrism.

27. Peter J. Gomes, "Best Sermon: A Pilgrim's Progress: The Bible as Civic Blueprint," *New York Times Magazine, New York Times on the Web,* Sunday, April 18, 1999.

28. See especially Frederick W. Robertson, *Sermons on Bible Subjects* (London: J. M. Dent & Sons; New York: E. P. Dutton & Co., 1906).

29. Ibid., "Solomon's Restoration," pp. 103-6.

30. Richard B. Hayes, *The Moral Vision of the New Testament,* part 2.

31. "A New Creed," *Voices United: The Hymn and Worship Book of the United Church of Canada* (Etobicoke, Ontario: The United Church Publishing House, 1996), p. 918.

32. Henry H. Mitchell, *Celebration and Experience in Preaching* (Nashville: Abingdon Press, 1990), p. 52.

33. Thomas G. Long, *The Witness of Preaching* (Louisville: Westminster/John Knox Press, 1989), p. 86.

34. See Wilson, *The Practice of Preaching* (Nashville: Abingdon Press, 1995), esp. pp. 117-18, 186, 263-83; and Wilson, *The Four Pages of the Sermon* (Nashville: Abingdon Press, 1999), pp. 56-57, 124-25, 149-51, 205-7, 226-28.

8. The Allegorical Sense in History

1. John Dominic Crossan, *In Parables: the Challenge of the Historical Jesus* (New York: Harper & Row, 1973), p. 8.

2. G. R. Evans, *The Language and Logic of the Bible: The Earlier Middle Ages* (Cambridge, UK: Cambridge University Press, 1984), p. 117.

3. Philo, *On Drunkenness,* trans. F. H. Colson and G. H. Whitaker, *Loeb Classical Library,* vol. 3 (London: Wm Heinemann; New York: G. P. Putnam's Sons, 1930), p. 395.

4. See Jacob Neusner, *What is Midrash? Guides to Biblical Scholarship* (Philadelphia: Fortress Press, 1987), pp. 7-8.

5. R. P. C. Hanson, *Allegory and Event: A Study of the Sources and Significance of Origen's Interpretation of Scripture* (London: SCM Press; Richmond, Va.: John Knox Press, 1959), pp.13-14.

6. Origen, "Homily VI," in *Homilies on Genesis and Exodus,* trans. Ronald E. Heine (Washington D. C.: The Catholic University of America, 1982), pp. 121-22.

7. See George Arthur Buttrick, et al., eds., *The Interpreter's Bible,* vol. 6 (New York: Abingdon Press, 1953), pp. 418-33.

8. Whitman, "Allegory," in T. V. F. Brogan, ed., *The New Princeton Handbook of Poetic Terms* (Princeton, N. J.: Princeton University Press, 1994), p. 8.

9. An argument can be made the other way as well, that analogy is the genus; and simile, metaphor, typology, and allegory are species. I choose the former alternative in part because I see allegory, not analogy, as the more precise paradigm of all interpretation. Some readers of the following examples might argue whether they are one figure or another and, again, an argument can be made both ways.

10. Some scholars defend this as typology since Paul does not explain who Sarah is. See "Allegory," *The Eerdmans Bible Dictionary,* Allen C. Myers, ed. (Grand Rapids, Mich.: William B. Eerdmans Publishing Co., 1987). The structure is nonetheless allegory since Sarah represents "the Jerusalem above" (Gal. 4:26).

11. See David Schnasa Jacobsen, *Preaching in the New Creation: The Promise of New Testament Apocalyptic Texts* (Louisville: Westminster John Knox Press, 1999), pp. 5, 67-71. He cautions preachers against trying to discern the reference of symbols in Revelation and to focus instead on what social reality the symbols employed by a text disclose in front of it.

12. For a common example of this tendency see for instance the Table of Parables in the NRSV (Grand Rapids, Mich.: Zondervan Publishing House, 1989) p. 1011; or Crossan, who discusses allegory only to drop it, *In Parables,* pp. 8-11. Crossan claims to have "no presumption that the term 'allegory' has a pejorative connotation or that allegory is a bad or inferior literary form, for Jesus or for anyone else," p. 10. He abandons the term allegory because he cannot determine "whether Jesus' stories *are* allegories in whole or in part, and if not, what are they?" p. 10.

13. James Samuel Preus, *From Shadow to Promise: Old Testament Interpretation from Augustine to the Young Luther* (Cambridge, Mass.: The Belknap Press of Harvard University Press, 1969), p. 43.

14. Andrew Louth for example argues against Cardinal Jean Daniélou's argument that "allegory is concerned with *words,* typology with *events;* allegory elides history, typology is rooted in history." Louth prefers de Lubac's distinction between *allegoria verbi,* that is a form of literary conceit and *allegoria facti,* that attempts to penetrate deeply into the mystery of Christ and is closely aligned with type. Andrew Louth, *Discerning the Mystery: An Essay on the Nature of Theology* (Oxford, UK: Clarendon Press, 1983), pp. 118-19.

15. Hanson, *Allegory and Event,* p. 128.

16. Ibid., p. 21.

17. Moisés Silva, *Has the Church Misread the Bible? The History of Interpretation in the Light of Current Issues* (Grand Rapids, Mich.: Zondervan Publishing House, 1987), p. 48.

18. See "An Ancient Christian Sermon Commonly Known as Second Clement," in *Apostolic Fathers,* 2d ed. (Grand Rapids, Mich.: Baker Press, 1979), pp. 68-78.

19. Stuart George Hall, ed., *Melito of Sardis:* On Pascha *and Fragments* (Oxford, UK: Clarendon Press, 1979), p. 5.

20. *The Revised Common Lectionary: The Consultation on Common Texts* (Nashville: Abingdon Press, 1992), p. 12.

21. Origen, "Homily VII," *Homilies on Genesis and Exodus*, pp. 131-32.

22. Robert W. Jenson, "Hermeneutics and the Life of the Church," in Carl E. Braaten and Robert W. Jenson, eds., *Reclaiming the Bible for the Church* (Grand Rapids, Mich. and Cambridge, UK: William B. Eerdmans Publishing Company, 1995), p. 96.

23. Karlfried Froehlich, ed., *Biblical Interpretation in the Early Church* (Philadelphia: Fortress Press, 1984), p. 19.

24. "Papyrus Michigan, Inv. 3718," in Froehlich, *Biblical Interpretation*, pp. 79-80. This catalogue gives examples of the various ways in which a term or phrase is used according to the senses.

> Thus, in a simple form of the *distinctio*, the idea of a bed is illustrated in one source as having several possibilities: In its literal or historical sense it means the "bed of Scripture" (Our bed is flourishing—Cant. 1:15). In its allegorical sense it means the "bed of contemplation" (There shall be two men in one bed—Luke 17:34); or it means "the bed of the church" (Three score valiant ones surrounded the bed of Solomon—Cant. 3:7). In its moral sense it means "bed of conscience" (Every night I will wash my bed—Psalm 6:7) or "bed of carnal pleasure" (You that sleep upon beds of ivory—Amos 6:4). In its anagogical sense it means "bed of eternal punishment" (I have made my bed in darkness—Job 17:13) or "bed of eternal blessedness" (My children are with me in bed—Luke 11:7).

25. Ibid., p. 79. See also Beryl Smalley and G. Lacombe, "The Lombard's Commentary on Isaias and other Fragments," *The New Scholasticism*, v (1931). Cited in Beryl Smalley, *The Study of the Bible in the Middle Ages* (Oxford, UK: The Clarendon Press, 1941), pp. 139-43.

26. Smalley, *Study of the Bible*, p. 113.

27. Ibid., p. 217.

28. Yaffe, "Interpretative Essay," in Thomas Aquinas, *The Literal Exposition on Job: A Scriptural Commentary Concerning Providence*, trans. Anthony Damico (Atlanta: Scholars Press, 1989), p. 9.

29. Martin Luther, "Sermon III," *A Selection of the Most Celebrated Sermons of Martin Luther* (n.p., Thomas Cowperthwaite & Co., 1817), p. 18.

30. Kenneth Hagen, "Luther, Martin (1483–1546)," Donald K. McKim, ed., *Historical Handbook of Major Biblical Interpreters* (Downer's Grove, Ill. and Leicester, England: InterVarsity Press, 1998), p. 218.

31. Jean Calvin, *Genesis*, 2 vols. in 1 (Carlisle, Penn.; Edinburgh, Scotland: The Banner of Truth Trust, 1975), p. 470.

32. Calvin, *Institutes*, in *Library of Christian Classics*, 6:1, p. 70.

33. David L. Puckett, *John Calvin's Exegesis of the Old Testament: Columbia Series in Reformed Theology* (Louisville: Westminster John Knox Press, 1995), pp. 105-32, esp. pp. 107, 110, 113.

34. Karl Barth, *Church Dogmatics*, vol. 4 *The Doctrine of Reconciliation Pt. 2* (Edinburgh, Scotland: T. & T. Clark, 1958), p. 21.

35. Louth, *Discerning the Mystery*, p. 96.

36. Augustine, *On Christian Doctrine*, trans. D. W. Robertson, Jr. (Indianapolis / New York: Bobbs-Merrill Co., 1958), III, 9:14.

37. Augustine, *City of God*, p. 307.

38. Ibid., p. 308.

39. James D. Smart, *The Interpretation of Scripture* (Philadelphia: The Westminster Press, 1961), p. 106.

40. Ibid., pp. 104-5.

41. Ibid., p. 132.

42. Ibid., pp. 107-8.

43. Brevard S. Childs, *Biblical Theology of the Old and New Testaments: Theological Reflection on the Christian Bible* (Minneapolis: Fortress Press, 1993), p. 14.

44. Louth, *Discerning the Mystery*, p. 129; see his chapter entitled, "Return to Allegory," pp. 96-131.

45. Frances Young, "Allegory and the Ethics of Reading," in Francis Watson, *The Open Text: New Directions for Biblical Studies?* (London: SCM Press, 1993), p. 118. See pp. 103-20.

46. David C. Steinmetz, "The Superiority of Pre-Critical Exegesis," *Theology Today*, 37:1 (April, 1980): p. 38.

47. Leander E. Keck, "The Premodern Bible in the Postmodern World," *Interpretation*, 50:2 (April, 1996): p. 139.

48. David L. Bartlett, *Between the Bible and the Church: New Methods for Biblical Preaching* (Nashville: Abingdon Press, 1999), p. 29.

49. Louth, *Discerning the Mystery*, pp. 97, 118-19.

50. David Buttrick, *Preaching the New and the Now* (Louisville: Westminster John Knox Press, 1998), pp. 85-86.

51. Jean Daniélou, *From Shadows to Reality: Studies in the Biblical Typology of the Fathers* (London: Burns & Oates, 1960).

52. Leonhard Goppelt, *Typos: The Typological Interpretation of the Old Testament in the New* (Grand Rapids, Mich.: William B. Eerdmans Publishing Company, 1982 [German 1938]).

53. Silva, *Has the Church Misread the Bible?* p. 71. He adds: "A rigorous definition of the allegorical method emphasizes its dehistoricizing, philosophizing [i.e., part of an involved philosophical system], arbitrary, and elitist [i.e., spiritual, mature believers] aspects," p. 74.

54. Justo L. González, "How the Bible Has Been Interpreted in Christian Tradition," in *The New Interpreter's Bible*, vol. 1 (Nashville: Abingdon Press, 1994), p. 92.

55. Silva, *Has the Church Misread the Bible?* pp. 101-2.

56. James Barr, "The Literal, the Allegorical, and Modern Biblical Scholarship," *JSOT* 44 (June, 1989): pp. 3-17. Childs responds to Barr that the similarity, "between traditional allegory and the work of some of these post-critical scholars... is superficial and is an almost accidental congruence arising from very different assumptions. Any identification obscures the fundamental differences which separate traditional allegory from modern exegesis." Brevard S. Childs, "Critical Reflections on James Barr's Understanding of the Literal and the Allegorical," in *JSOT* 46 (February, 1990): p. 8.

57. Louth, *Discerning the Mystery*, pp. 97-98.

9. Allegory, Anagogy, and Preaching

1. David E. Reid, "The Problem with Allegory in Preaching," *Preaching*, vol. 11, no. 3 (November/December, 1995): p. 68.

2. See Wilson, *The Practice of Preaching* (Nashville: Abingdon Press, 1995), esp. pp. 238-62.

3. See Wilson, "Biblical Studies and Preaching," in Thomas G. Long and Edward Farley, eds., *Preaching As a Theological Task: World, Gospel, Scripture* (Louisville: Westminster John Knox Press, 1996), pp. 137-49, esp. p. 142.

4. Stephen Farris, *Preaching That Matters: The Bible and Our Lives* (Louisville: Westminster John Knox Press, 1998), pp. 75-124. He discusses potential analogy in Luke 7:36-50, pp. 88-92.

5. Northrop Frye, *Anatomy of Criticism: Four Essays* (Princeton, N.J.: Princeton University Press, 1957), p. 89.

6. Frances Young, "Allegory and the Ethics of Reading," in Francis Watson, *The Open Text: New Directions for Biblical Studies?* (London: SCM Press, 1993), p. 117.

7. Whitman, "Allegory," in T. V. F. Brogan, ed., *The New Princeton Handbook of Poetic Terms* (Princeton, N. J.: Princeton University Press, 1994), p. 7.

8. On this point see Kathryn E. Tanner, "Theology and the Plain Sense," in Garrett W. I. Green, ed., *Scriptural Authority and Narrative Interpretation: Essays on the Occasion of the Sixty-Fifth Birthday of Hans W. Frei* (Minneapolis: Fortress Press, 1987), pp. 72-73.

9. Calvin: *Commentaries on the Book of the Prophet Daniel, vol. 1*, trans. Thomas Myers (Grand Rapids, Mich.: Wm. B. Eerdmans Publishing Company, 1948), 4:10-16, p. 257.

10. See esp. Wilson, *The Practice of Preaching*, pp. 146-76.

11. See Krister Stendahl, "Biblical Theology, Contemporary," in *The Interpreter's Dictionary of the Bible*, vol. 1, ed. George Arthur Buttrick, et al. (Nashville: Abingdon Press, 1962), 418-31, esp. p. 422.

12. Farris, *Preaching That Matters*, pp. 92-93.

13. Karl Barth, *Church Dogmatics*, vol. 4, *The Doctrine of Reconciliation*, pt. 2 (Edinburgh, Scotland: T & T Clark, 1958), p. 22.

14. David L. Bartlett, *Between the Bible and the Church: New Methods for Biblical Preaching* (Nashville: Abingdon Press, 1999), p. 31.

15. Lancelot Andrewes, "Of the Resurrection," in *Andrewes' Sermons*, vol. 2 of *Library of Anglo-Catholic Theology* (Oxford: John Henry Parker, 1841), p. 396.

16. Bartlett, *Between the Bible and the Church*, pp. 16-36.

17. Robert W. Jenson, "Hermeneutics and the Life of the Church," in Carl E. Braaten and Robert W. Jenson, eds., *Reclaiming the Bible for the Church* (Grand Rapids, Mich. and Cambridge, UK: William B. Eerdmans Publishing Company, 1995), p. 97. Jenson alludes to Childs in this quotation.

18. Sandra M. Schneiders, *The Revelatory Text: Interpreting the New Testament as Sacred Scripture* (New York: HarperSanFrancisco, 1991), p. 163.

19. Ibid.

20. Sidney Greidanus, *Preaching From the Old Testament: A Contemporary Hermeneutical Method* (Grand Rapids, Mich.: William B. Eerdmans Publishing Company, 1999), pp. 215-25, 319-44.

21. Augustine, "Christmas," in *St. Augustine: Sermons for Christmas and Epiphany,* vol. 15 of *Ancient Christian Writers,* trans. Thomas Comerford Lawler (Westminster, Md.: Newman Press; London: Longmans Green & Co., 1952), p. 85.

22. Marcus J. Borg, *Meeting Jesus Again for the First Time: The Historical Jesus and the Heart of Contemporary Faith* (New York: HarperSanFrancisco, 1994), pp. 121-33.

23. Moisés Silva, *Has the Church Misread the Bible? The History of Interpretation in the Light of Current Issues* (Grand Rapids, Mich.: Zondervan Publishing House, 1987), pp. 63, 66-67.

24. Edward Farley, "Preaching the Bible and Preaching the Gospel," *Theology Today* 51:1 (April, 1994): pp. 90-103, esp. p. 103.

25. Frances Young comments, "For some kind of allegory is involved in any hermeneutic, and the curious Two-Nature or sacramental possibilities that emerge from treating the biblical texts as Word of God seem to me to have been submerged by most modern readings." Frances Young, "Allegory and the Ethics of Reading," in Watson, *Open Text,* p. 117.

26. Robert W. Jenson, "Hermeneutics and the Life of the Church," in Braaten, et al., *Reclaiming,* p. 97.

27. See Paul Scott Wilson, *The Four Pages of the Sermon: A Guide to Biblical Preaching* (Nashville: Abingdon Press, 1999), pp. 44-47, 74-75, 92-93, 147-49, 172, 179-80, 210.

28. Guibert DeNogent, "A Book about the Way a Sermon ought to Be Given," trans. Joseph M. Miller, *Today's Speech* 17:4 (Nov. 1969): p. 49.

29. James Samuel Preus, *From Shadow to Promise: Old Testament Interpretation from Augustine to the Young Luther* (Cambridge, Mass.: The Belknap Press of Harvard University Press, 1969), p. 58.

30. David Buttrick, *Preaching the New and the Now* (Louisville: Westminster John Knox Press, 1998), pp. 22, 132, 141.

31. Karl Barth, *The Epistle to the Romans,* trans. Edwyn C. Hoskyns (London / Oxford/New York: Oxford University Press, 1975 [1933]), p. 500.

32. Reinhold Niebuhr, *The Nature and Destiny of Man: A Christian Interpretation,* vol. 2 (New York: Charles Scribner's Sons, 1949), p. 294.

33. Shirley C. Guthrie, *Christian Doctrine,* rev. ed. (Louisville: Westminster John Knox Press, 1994), pp. 381-86.

34. Cited by Carter Lindberg, *The European Reformations* (Oxford, UK and Cambridge, Mass.: Blackwell Publishers, 1996), p. 133.

35. Charles H. Spurgeon, "Christ the Destroyer of Death," in E. J. Wheeler, ed., *Pulpit and Grave: A Volume of Funeral Sermons and Addresses From Leading Pulpits of America, England, Germany, and France* (New York and London: Funk and Wagnalls Co., 1894), p. 47.

36. I. S. Spencer, "Sorrow for the Death of Friends," in Wheeler, *Pulpit and Grave,* p. 111.

37. John Donne, "Sermon No. 10," *The Sermons of John Donne,* vol. 5, eds. George R. Potter and Evelyn M. Simpson (Berkeley and Los Angeles: University of

California Press, 1962), p. 215.

38. Robertson, "The Israelite's Grave in a Foreign Land," Frederick W. Robertson, *Sermons on Bible Subjects* (London: J. M. Dent & Sons; New York: E. P. Dutton & Co., 1906), p. 51.

39. Arthur John Gossip, "But When Life Tumbles In, What Then?" in his *The Hero in Thy Soul: Being an Attempt to Face Life Gallantly* (Edinburgh, Scotland: T & T Clark, 1928), pp. 114-15.

40. Martin Luther King, Jr., "Conscience for Change: Massey Lectures," 7th Ser. (Toronto: Canadian Broadcasting Corporation, 1967), pp. 44-46.

41. Elizabeth Achtemeier, "Of Children and Streets and the Kingdom," in Thomas G. Long and Cornelius Plantinga, Jr., eds., *A Chorus of Witnesses: Model Sermons for Today's Preacher* (Grand Rapids, Mich.: William B. Eerdmans Publishing Company, 1994), p. 70.

42. Cornelius Plantinga, Jr., "In the Interim Between Two Advents," *The Christian Century* (December 6, 2000): p. 1272.

Appendix: God's Medicine

1. Tex Sample related this story of himself in an address to the Academy of Homiletics, Dallas, Perkins School of Theology, Southern Methodist University, December 1, 2000.

Index

Abraham, 117, 125, 128, 150
Absalom, 47, 96
Achtemeier, Elizabeth, 30, 65, 159
Adam, 76-77, 105
Adams, A. K., 175 n. 46
Akiba, Rabbi, 117
Alan of Lille, 95
Allegory
  abuse of Scripture and, 14, 40
  anagogy and, 89-90, 155-63
  analogy and, 148-52
  anti-Semitism and, 14, 112
  bad, 112-13, 114, 125, 130, 144-45
  connections made by, 13, 14, 144
  diachronic, 125
  dishonesty of, 133
  doctrine and, 85, 116, 126, 129-31, 152-55
  good, 112-14, 116, 130, 138, 144-45
  history and, 125, 134, 135, 137
  Jesus' use of, 119-22, 131-32
  metaphor as. *See* Metaphor
  as multipoint grid. *See* Multipoint grid
  mythology and, 114
  as opposed to literal, 23
  as a paradigm of interpretation, 138-42
  prejudice and, 14
  preservation of Scripture by, 13-14,
  sense of, 16, 88-90, 91, 95, 112-64
  typology and, 122-26
Allen, Ronald J., 177 n. 19
Ambrose of Milan, 93
Anagogy, 16, 85, 88-90, 91, 95, 116, 122, 137, 155-63
Analogy, 58, 87, 94, 95, 113, 118, 138-41, 148-52
Anderson, James, 174 n. 37
Andrew of St. Victor, 96, 127

Andrewes, Lancelot, 146
Anselm, 95
Arafat, Yasir, 159
Aristotle, 25, 26, 50, 141
Athanasius of Alexandria, 170 n. 1
Auerbach, Erich, 171 n. 9
Augustine of Dacia, 16, 83, 88, 91
Augustine of Hippo, 10, 15, 29, 71, 95
  and the Literal sense, 41, 42, 47, 89, 170 n. 7
  and the Moral sense, 96, 99
  and Allegory, 130, 149-50
Aulen, Gustaf, 151
Authors, biblical, 51, 63, 66

Bachmann, E. Theodore, 173 n. 29
Barak, Ehud, 159
Barr, James, 134
Barth, Karl, 30, 58, 65, 132, 156
  and bad allegory, 128, 144-45
Bartlett, David L., 54, 65, 133, 146, 147
Bible
  authority of the, 12, 62
  as the church's book, 10
  exegesis of the. *See* Exegesis
  God in the. *See* God
  as an image in the sermon, 79-80
  preaching the, 23
  revelation in the, 10, 18, 46, 51, 66
  as Scripture, 63-65
  theology and, 34, 57-58
  translation of, 24-25, 32
  unity of, 55, 58, 132, 148, 153
  as Word of God, 23, 26, 27, 40, 41, 53, 62, 67
Biblical criticism
  canonical, 53
  historical. *See* Historical criticism
  homiletical. *See* Homiletical criticism